DRIVER'S HANDBOOK

D1104894

─── **LES PUBLICATIONS DU QUÉBEC** ───
1500 D, rue Jean-Talon Nord, Québec (Québec) G1N 2E5

SALES AND DISTRIBUTION
Telephone: 418 643-5150, Toll free, 1 800 463-2100
Fax: 418 643-6177, Toll free, 1 800 561-3479
Internet: www.publicationsduquebec.gouv.qc.ca

Library and Archives Canada Cataloguing in Publication

Main entry under title :

    Driver's handbook
    Translation of: Guide de la route.
    Includes index.

    ISSN 1182-8722
    ISBN 978-2-551-19725-5

    1. Traffic safety - Québec (Province) - Handbooks, manuals, etc. 2. Automobile driving - Québec (Province) - Handbooks, manuals, etc. 3. Traffic regulations - Québec (Province) - Handbooks, manuals, etc. 4. Traffic signs and signals - Québec (Province) - Handbooks, manuals, etc. I. Société de l'assurance automobile du Québec.

KEQ590.S4213   343.71409'46   C91-082284-0

LES PUBLICATIONS DU QUÉBEC

DRIVER'S HANDBOOK

Québec ✚✚✚

Edition produced by:
Les Publications du Québec
1500 D, rue Jean-Talon Nord,
1st floor
Québec (Québec) G1N 2E5

Project officer
Pierre Fortier

Art direction
Lucie Pouliot

Production
Laurent Langlois

Illustrations
Bertrand Lachance

Graphic design and layout
Deschamps Design

This publication was prepared by
the Société de l'assurance automobile
du Québec in cooperation with
the Service des technologies
d'exploitation of Transport Québec.

Researched and written by:
Micheline Briand,
Service des usagers de la route

With the cooperation of:
Claude Nazair,
Ministère des Transports

Direction des communications
Diane Godbout

English translation
Elizabeth Doyle

Legal deposit – 2006
Bibliothèque et Archives nationales du Québec
National Library and Archives Canada
ISBN 978-2-551-19725-5
ISSN 1182-8722
© Gouvernement du Québec – 2006

INTRODUCTION

This publication, intended for road users, condenses the *Highway Safety Code* and attendant regulations. It reiterates their major provisions, reminds the reader of the rules of the road and offers practical advice.

All road users, whether they are pedestrians, cyclists, motor vehicle operators or passengers, will find their rights and obligations set forth in this Handbook.

This edition includes the particular requirements of each class of licence, the terms for obtaining a disabled parking permit, new measures that concern the driving of a motor vehicle under the influence of alcohol, including the obligation, at the first offence, to submit to a summary evaluation conducted by a specialist from the Fédération québécoise des centres de réadaptation pour les personnes alcooliques et toxicomanes for individuals with addictions, and requiring the mandatory use, in some cases, of an alcohol ignition interlock device before a licence can be reinstated. The Handbook also reviews standards for the installation, replacement and deactivation of air bags.

The chapter on road signs and traffic signals provides descriptions of each type of sign and explains their use.

The traffic rules chapter details the fine points of turning right at a red light. It presents new standards concerning the mandatory use of a child restraint device adapted to a child's size and provides a brief explanation of air bags, conditions for use of electric power-assisted bicycles on public roads and reinforced safety rules for the use of foot scooters on roadways. It also lists safety tips for drivers approaching a road work area, rules for travel on logging roads, provides an overview of heavy vehicle use and urges drivers to take other road users into consideration to make roads safer.

For legal purposes, the reader is urged to refer to the official text of the legislation.

TABLE OF CONTENTS

Chapter 1

THE DRIVER

*T*o operate a motor vehicle on a public roadway in Québec, an individual must hold a licence of the class corresponding to the type of vehicle. Depending on which provisions of the Highway Safety Code apply to the person's situation, the Société de l'assurance automobile du Québec (SAAQ) is the agency which issues a learner's licence, a probationary licence, a regular driver's licence or a restricted licence.

Over 4,400,000 Quebecers hold a driver's licence.

Having a driver's licence is not an inherent right. Getting and keeping a licence depends on meeting requirements and specific conditions. A licence is also subject to withdrawal when a holder's behaviour or state of health represents a danger to other road users.

Drivers must take their state of health into consideration and be aware of how this could influence their driving.

THE DRIVER'S LICENCE

A FIRST LICENCE

A first driver's licence is issued for the operation of a passenger vehicle (class 5 licence). A Quebecer may qualify for a first driver's licence after holding a learner's licence, and if age 16 through 24, a probationary licence.

BASIC REQUIREMENTS

To obtain a driver's licence for a passenger vehicle, a person must be at least age 16. The written consent of a parental authority (father, mother, guardian) is required for persons under age 18.

Applicants must also present two pieces of identification: the first must be an official birth certificate issued by the Directeur de l'état civil du Québec or a civil authority recognized elsewhere in Canada, a certificate of Canadian citizenship, a Permanent Resident Card or a Canadian passport. The second piece of identification may be a provincial health insurance card.

KNOWLEDGE REQUIREMENT

Prospective licence holders must first acquire a certain amount of theoretical knowledge about the *Highway Safety Code*, road signs, traffic signals and techniques before driving a passenger vehicle. This theory can be learned:

- by studying reference material prepared by the Société de l'assurance automobile, including this Handbook, which contains information for prospective licence holders on driving techniques, and the manual entitled *Driving a Passenger Vehicle*. These documents are sold in Publications du Québec outlets and bookstores throughout Québec;
- by taking a driving school course.

CHOOSING A DRIVING SCHOOL

Driving school courses are optional. However, if you complete a practical course at a driving school recognized by CAA-Québec or the Québec Safety League, you can cut four months off the minimum length of the training period, which will be 8 months instead of a year from the date a learner's licence is issued. Under the *Highway Safety Code*, a learner who has passed a course can then take the Société's road test.

For information on recognized driving schools, contact:

CAA-Québec
444, rue Bouvier
Québec (Québec) G2J 1E3
Montréal: (514) 861-7575
Elsewhere in Québec: 1 800 924-0708

Québec Safety League
Association québécoise du transport et des routes
533, rue Ontario Est, suite 206
Montréal (Québec) H2L 1N8
Montréal: (514) 523-6444

LEARNER'S LICENCE

A person must hold a learner's licence before learning to drive. A learner must:

- certify on a medical declaration that he/she is able to drive without risk to public safety and must meet medical requirements;
- pass the Société's vision test;

- pass a knowledge test, which concerns the *Highway Safety Code*, road signs, traffic signals and techniques of driving a passenger vehicle.

It is possible to rewrite the test in the event of failure. The applicant rewrites only those parts of the test he/she has failed. However, applicants must wait a minimum of 7 days between tests.

PRACTICE

A learner's licence allows its holder to acquire the knowledge and skills necessary to drive a passenger vehicle on the road.

When practising on the roadway, a person who has held a valid driver's licence to drive a passenger vehicle for at least 2 years must accompany a learner. This person must be seated next to the learner and be prepared to provide him/her with assistance and advice. A person who holds a probationary licence is not qualified to accompany a learner during practice driving.

During the learning period, the holder of a learner's licence is subject to particular rules. The maximum number of demerit points is 4 and it is compulsory to maintain a zero blood alcohol level. Maintaining a zero blood alcohol level means that a learner is prohibited from driving after having consumed any alcohol at all.

ROAD TEST

To qualify for a road test, the applicant must have held a learner's licence for at least 12 months, or 8 months after completing a driving course at a recognized school.

A road test enables the Société to evaluate a prospective driver's knowledge and skills. During a road test, the applicant will be required to perform manoeuvres relevant to roadway driving: driving in a straight line, taking a curve, stopping or going through an intersection, turning, changing lanes and backing up.

During a road test, an applicant must:

- obey traffic rules;
- demonstrate an ability to adapt to different driving situations;
- show safe driving techniques;
- follow the examiner's instructions.

If an applicant fails a road test, he or she must wait a minimum of 21 days between tests.

GETTING A LICENCE

Once a road test has been passed, a licence applicant age 16 through 24 is issued a probationary licence. Drivers age 25 and over are issued a driver's licence.

At a Société service outlet, a driver is issued a temporary licence which he/she must keep until a plastic licence bearing his/her photograph is received by mail, usually within 10 days. Upon receipt of the photo licence, the driver must destroy the temporary licence.

••• Probationary Licence •••

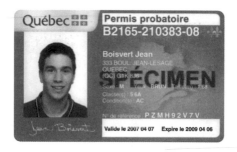

A probationary licence is valid for two years or until age 25, whichever comes first. A probationary licence holder who turns 25 within the two-year period may obtain a driver's licence at a Société service outlet.

Probationary licence holders are subject to the same restrictions that apply to a learner (maintaining a zero blood alcohol level and a maximum of 4 demerit points). A probationary licence holder is not allowed to serve as the accompanying rider for someone who holds a learner's or probationary licence.

••• Driver's Licence •••

To receive a driver's licence, a new driver must pay the amount determined under regulation. These amounts include remittance fees to the Ministère des Finances du Québec, administration fees and an insurance premium under the public plan.

Driver's licence holders are subject to a legal blood alcohol limit of .08% (80 mg of alcohol per 100 ml of blood) and a maximum of 15 demerit points. Failure to comply will result in licence revocation.

LICENCE CLASSES

There are twelve classes of licences in Québec. Each class authorizes the holder to drive a category of vehicle on a Québec road.

Once a person has been issued a licence to drive a particular class of vehicle, other classes of vehicles are generally authorized, as shown in the following table.

LICENCE UPGRADE

Changing one's licence class to another is not done simply on request. Before applying for a particular class, a driver must meet certain pre-conditions, which may require a driving experience of 1 to 3 years or a health care professional's report on fitness to drive.

To get a licence, an applicant must go to a SAAQ service centre to take the knowledge and road test, after passing an initial vision test.

Some classes also require the applicant to hold a learner's licence or probationary licence for a certain period.

These principal requirements are detailed in the following table.

Specific information on licence classes can be found in brochures available from Société service centres, through its information line (1 800 361-7620) or, in French, at the Web site (www.saaq.gouv.qc.ca).

LICENCE CLASSES AUTHORIZING THE HOLDER TO DRIVE HEAVY VEHICLES

CLASS		Vehicles Authorized	Requirements
1		A combination of vehicles, including: • a tractor semi-trailer: a road tractor (truck having no load space, equipped with a trailer hitch) towing a semi-trailer; • a tractor semi-trailer combination: a straight truck (vehicle authorized in class 3) towing a trailer whose net weight is at least 2,000 kg; • a double road train: a road tractor towing two semi-trailers. **Classes included:** 2, 3, 4A, 4B, 4C, 5, 6D and 8	• Three years' experience as the holder of a class 5 licence or 2 years if the applicant has successfully completed training in a centre recognized by the SAAQ that includes 300 hours of driving a vehicle combination on a public road. • Three months' experience as the holder of a class 1 learner's licence or 1 month if the applicant is registered in a truck driving training program authorized by the Ministere de l'Education as a requirement for a vocational diploma.
2		A bus with a seating capacity for more than 24 passengers. **Classes included:** 3, 4A, 4B, 4C, 5, 6D and 8	• Two years' experience as the holder of a class 5 licence. • Three months' experience as the holder of a class 2 learner's licence.

CLASS		Vehicles Authorized	Requirements
3		A straight-body truck designed to carry goods, including: • a truck with 3 or more axles; or • a truck with 2 axles and whose net weight is 4,500 kg or over. **Classes included:** 4A, 4B, 4C, 5, 6D and 8	• Two years' experience as the holder of a class 5 licence. • Three months' experience as the holder of a class 3 learner's licence.

To obtain a class 1, 2 or 3[1] learner's licence, an applicant must:

• have a driving record with fewer than 4 demerit points;

• not have had his/her licence revoked or suspended for demerit points or a driving-related *Criminal Code* offence within the previous two years;

• provide a medical examination or health assessment report showing fitness to drive.

Tests

Successfully pass a vision test, knowledge test, pre-trip inspection test and road test with the vehicle in question.

Endorsements for classes 1, 2 or 3

Holders of a class 1, 2 or 3 driver's licence must have an endorsement on their licence certifying authorization to drive certain heavy vehicles. These endorsements are indicated on the licence:

- **F** attests that the person is allowed to drive a heavy vehicle equipped with air brakes;
- **M** attests that the person is allowed to drive a heavy vehicle equipped with a manual transmission;
- **T** attests that the person is allowed to drive a double road train, requiring a special travel permit. This endorsement only applies to class 1 and requires the holder to have held this class of licence for at least 5 years.

A licence endorsement also requires that the holder pass a specific test.

---

1. Further information on these licence classes is contained in the brochure *Prospective Heavy Vehicle Driver*, available through SAAQ service centres, the information line (1 800 361-7620) or the Web site (www.saaq.gouv.qc.ca).

CLASS		Vehicles Authorized	Requirements
4A		An emergency vehicle (ex. ambulance, police vehicle, fire truck). **Classes included:** 4B, 4C, 5, 6D and 8	• Two years' experience as the holder of a class 5 licence or hold a class 5 licence and have passed an emergency vehicle driving course given by the Québec police training institute or its equivalent. • At the time of application, submit a medical examination or health assessment report completed by a physician showing fitness to drive. • Pass a vision and knowledge test.
4B		Minibus: passenger motor vehicle with 2 single-wheel axles and no more than 5 rows of seats, or a bus with a seating capacity for 24 or fewer passengers. **Classes included:** 4C, 5, 6D and 8	• One year of experience as the holder of a class 5 licence. • At the time of application, submit a medical examination or health assessment report completed by a physician showing fitness to drive. • Pass a vision and knowledge test.

CLASS		Vehicles Authorized	Requirements
4C		Taxicab **Classes included:** 5, 6D and 8	• One year of experience as the holder of a class 5 licence. • At the time of application, submit a medical examination or health assessment report completed by a physician showing fitness to drive. • No prior conviction within the last 5 years for an offence related to operation of a taxi. • A person must hold a taxi permit, in accordance with the *Transportation by Taxi Act* and *Regulation.* Transport Québec has prepared the Québec taxi driver's hand-book, which provides more information. • Pass a vision and knowledge test.

CLASS		Vehicles Authorized	Requirements
5		• A passenger vehicle (automobile or mini-van) or truck with 2 axles whose net weight is less than 4,500 kg; • A motor home; • A tool vehicle: motor vehicle in which the work station is contained within the driver's compartment. The vehicle is manufactured to carry out a task and designed to travel at a maximum speed of 70 km/h; • A service vehicle: vehicle equipped to supply, repair or tow motor vehicles. Also authorized is any vehicle covered by this class hauling a trailer or in the case of a motor home, another vehicle. **Classes included:** 6D, 8	• Applicants must be age 16 or over. The written consent of a person with parental authority is required if the applicant is a minor. • One year of experience as the holder of a learner's licence, or 8 months in the case of a person who has passed a driving course at a recognized school. • Pass a vision test, knowledge exam and road test. • Hold a probationary licence valid for 2 years or until age 25.
6A		Any motorcycle. **Classes included:** 6B, 6C, 6D, 8	See below.

CLASS		Vehicles Authorized	Requirements
6B		A motorcycle with a cylinder size of 400 cc or less. **Classes included:** 6C, 6D, 8	See below.
6C		A motorcycle with a cylinder size of 125 cc or less. **Classes included:** 6D, 8	See below.

REQUIREMENTS FOR A MOTORCYCLE (Classes 6A, 6B, 6C)

Applicants for a licence to operate a motorcycle must go through the following steps and meet the demands of each.

To obtain a CLASS 6R LEARNER'S LICENCE for a motorcycle – this licence allows motorcycle operation only for purposes of a driving course or a Société road test.

Applicants must:

- Be age 16 or over. The written consent of a person with parental authority is required if the applicant is a minor.

- Pass a vision test and knowledge exam on the *Highway Safety Code*, road signs and traffic signals and techniques for operating a motorcycle (an applicant who fails must wait a minimum of 28 days between tests).

To obtain a CLASS 6A LEARNER'S LICENCE – this licence allows operation of a motorcycle with an accompanying rider on another motorcycle.

Applicants must:

- Have passed a motorcycle driving course given at a school recognized by CAA-Québec or the Quebec Safety League.

- Hold a class 6R learner's licence for at least 1 month.

- Pass a test on a closed track (an applicant who fails must wait a minimum of 14 days between tests).

To obtain a class 6A, 6B OR 6C DRIVER'S LICENCE.

- Hold a class 6A learner's licence for at least 7 months.

- Pass a road test using the type of motorcycle that corresponds to the licence sought (an applicant who fails must wait a minimum of 56 days between tests).

- Hold, if the applicant does not have a class 5 driver's licence, a probationary licence for 2 years or until age 25 (during this period, the rule of maintaining a zero blood alcohol level applies and no more than 4 demerit points are allowed).

CLASS		Vehicles Authorized	Requirements
6D		Moped or motorized scooter	• Applicants must be at least age 14. The written consent of a parental authority is required if the applicant is a minor. • Do the exercises and submit the Home Study Program answer sheet from the *Guide for Moped and Scooter Operators* available through the Société's service centres. • Pass a vision test and knowledge exam.
8		Farm Tractor	• Applicants must be at least age 16. The consent of a parental authority is required if the applicant is a minor. • Pass a vision test and knowledge exam.

HEALTH REQUIREMENTS

Driving safely not only demands know-how and skills, but also a state of health that is consistent with the operation of a particular type of vehicle and its use.

Certain illnesses, disabilities or situations can interfere with a person's ability to drive safely. The *Regulation respecting access to driving a road vehicle in connection with the health of drivers* describes these conditions. The most common include sight disorders, cardiovascular diseases, mental illness, alcoholism, drug dependency and medication, epilepsy, diabetes, kidney and lung diseases.

At the time of applying for a licence or on renewal, everyone has an obligation to advise the SAAQ of any health condition that might affect driving, and accordingly must fill out and sign the Declaration of Illness or Impairment form. The SAAQ must also be informed of any change in a licence holder's state of health within 30 days.

A person's particular health condition may affect eligibility for classes of licences and restrict driving privileges. The most common situation is one in which the Société issues a licence with conditions:

- requiring the driver to wear eyeglasses, contact lenses or a hearing aid;
- requiring the installation of equipment in the vehicle for driving;
- limiting the time of day, period and area for driving;
- limiting the types of vehicles;
- requiring the presence of another licence holder;
- allowing the person to drive only a vehicle that is equipped with an alcohol ignition interlock device.

One or more of the following conditions may appear on a driver's licence:

A	Must wear eyeglasses or contact lenses while driving
B	Must drive only during the daytime
C	Must wear a hearing aid when driving
G	Must undergo a medical examination or health assessment on renewal
H	Must drive only a vehicle with a net weight of less than 2,500 kg
I	Must drive only a vehicle equipped with an alcohol ignition interlock device
J	Must drive only a vehicle equipped with an automatic transmission
K	Must drive only a vehicle equipped with power steering
L	Must drive only a vehicle equipped with power brakes
N	Must wear a safety harness when driving
P	Must drive only a vehicle equipped with hand-operated controls
Q	Must drive only a vehicle equipped with a manual dimmer switch
R	Must drive only a vehicle equipped with an accelerator on the left
S	Is subject to medical restrictions as indicated
V	Must drive only a vehicle equipped with controls adapted to his/her disability

The Société may require a driver to undergo a proficiency test, medical examination or health assessment in the following cases:

- the licence holder is 70 years of age;
- the licence authorizes him/her to drive a tractor semi-trailer, tractor-trailer, straight-body truck, road train, bus or minibus, emergency vehicle or taxicab;
- the driver has not undergone an examination within the last ten years;
- the Société has reasonable grounds to verify the driver's health or driving behaviour on public roads.

Proficiency exams (knowledge or road test) may be required of a person who wishes to change a licence class. A medical examination or health assessment may be required before a condition on the licence can be changed.

The Société may also require a licence holder to submit a periodic medical or optometric report where a disorder or impairment requires a periodic follow-up.

The Société may suspend the licence or licence class of any driver who:

- makes a false health declaration or fails to declare a health condition;
- refuses to undergo a medical examination or health assessment or fails to submit the related report;
- refuses to take or fails a proficiency test;
- is afflicted with an illness or disability that could jeopardize roadway safety.

RESPONSIBILITIES OF A DRIVER

Anyone operating a motor vehicle on a public roadway must carry a valid licence bearing his/her signature. A driver must respect the conditions indicated on his/her licence. A law enforcement officer may seize the vehicle of a driver who does not hold a licence for the class of vehicle driven and may impound it for thirty days.

A driver must also have all the documents related to the vehicle, that is:

- a valid registration certificate for the vehicle;
- proof of insurance coverage or solvency;
- a lease contract (original or copy) for a vehicle rented for less than a 1 year period;
- written proof of the period of the loan of a vehicle by a car dealer.

A vehicle driver or owner without third-party liability insurance who becomes involved in an accident causing more than $500 in property damage is subject to licence suspension (driver's licence, probationary licence or learner's licence). The operation of any vehicle registered in that person's name is also prohibited, until the SAAQ is provided with a payment guarantee or proof of settlement covering the damage.

The obligation of carrying documents not only applies to travel on a public roadway; some are required for private roads open to public traffic, on logging roads and on shopping centre parking lots.

For holders of licence classes 1, 2 or 3, other documentation may be required, such as the driving and duty time log, pre-trip inspection report or certain certificates, depending on the type of load or services provided.

A law enforcement officer may require a driver to produce any of these documents for examination.

ONLY ONE LICENCE

It is an offence to hold more than one valid driver's licence, probationary licence or learner's licence issued by the Société or another authority in Canada or the U.S. for the same class. It is also an offence to lend a licence or knowingly give false or misleading information to obtain one.

CORRECT ADDRESS

The address that appears on a licence must be the holder's principal place of residence. The holder must advise the Société of a change of address, following which the Société will send a confirmation, which must be kept with the licence.

Under threat of penalties set forth in the *Highway Safety Code*, a licence holder must notify the Société of a change of address within 30 days by mail, in person at a service centre or by telephone at 1 800 361-7620.

LICENCE REPLACEMENT

The holder of a licence that has been lost, stolen, destroyed, damaged or on which information has become inaccurate must request a replacement from the Société. The Société will replace the licence on payment of the required fee and presentation of two pieces of identification.

RENEWING A LICENCE

Although a plastic licence with a photo is intended to last 4 years, the holder is required to pay a licence fee every 2 years, even where he/she fails to receive notice. Insurance premiums on the licence are set according to the number of demerit points entered on the holder's driving record. In the absence of payment, the licence holder is not allowed to drive. Driving with an invalid licence is an offence punishable by a minimum fine of $300 and additional penalties.

Once a licence has been invalid for at least 3 years, the person must pass a knowledge test and a road test to drive again.

HEALTH DECLARATION

A licence holder must declare any diseases or disorders when the Société asks for information on his/her health, and must fill out and sign the declaration form when applying for a licence or upon its renewal. Licence holders must also advise the Société of any change in their health.

RESPONSIBILITIES OF PERSONS FROM OUTSIDE QUEBEC

NEW RESIDENTS

A newly arrived resident of Québec may drive a passenger vehicle for 90 days provided he/she holds a valid driver's licence.

After 90 days, he or she must apply for a Quebec licence, which may or may not require a proficiency exam:

- Any person who holds a driver's licence for a passenger vehicle issued by a Canadian province or territory, the U.S., Belgium, South Korea, France, Japan, or certain OECD member countries may, upon taking up residence in Québec, exchange this licence for a class 5 licence issued by the Société.

- For a person who takes up residence in Québec and does not come from one of the jurisdictions identified above, the conditions vary according to the number of years the person has held a valid driver's licence corresponding to a class 5:
  - if the applicant has held a licence for at least 1 year at the time he/she takes up residence in Québec, he/she must pass a knowledge exam and road test before the Société can issue a licence;
  - if the applicant has held a licence for less than 1 year, the licence is not recognized by the Société; he/she is therefore subject to the same requirements as applicants for their first driver's licence.

Details on licence exchange may be obtained by contacting the nearest Société service centre, customer information line (514 954-7771 or 1 888 356-6616) or, in French, at the Web site (www.saaq.gouv.qc.ca).

NON-RESIDENTS

A non-resident may operate a motor vehicle in Québec for a period of not more than 6 consecutive months without obtaining a Québec licence. A non-resident must, however, hold a valid driver's licence issued by a jurisdiction outside Québec which grants the same right to Québec residents, must drive only those vehicles covered by the licence and must respect any attendant conditions.

A student, co-operant or trainee who is a non-resident and studying at an educational institution in Québec, is exempt from having to obtain a Québec licence to drive a passenger vehicle for the period of studies or training, providing the issuing jurisdiction grants the same right to Québec residents.

A non-resident who holds a valid international driver's licence issued by his/her country of origin may for the period of its validity drive the motor vehicles authorized by the holder's regular licence, which must be valid and kept with the international driver's licence for presentation.

A REVOKED OR SUSPENDED LICENCE

To revoke a licence means to withdraw the driving privilege. A person whose licence has been revoked is not allowed to operate a motor vehicle and must comply with conditions prescribed by the *Highway Safety Code* before being issued a licence again.

A licence suspension is by nature temporary. A person whose right to obtain a licence has been suspended cannot obtain any licence from the Société for a fixed period of time.

Revocation of a licence, its suspension or suspension of the right to obtain a licence can occur:

- as a result of an unpaid fine for an offence under the *Highway Safety Code* or a municipal traffic or parking bylaw;

- for an accumulation of demerit points due to *Highway Safety Code* offences;

- following a conviction of a driving-related offence under the *Criminal Code*.

The Société is notified of traffic offences that are committed by drivers in another Canadian province or a U.S. state with which Québec has a reciprocity agreement and demerit points are entered on the driver's record as if the offence had taken place in Québec.

SUSPENSION FOR AN UNPAID FINE

Drivers who do not pay fines for offences under the *Highway Safety Code* or a municipal traffic bylaw will have their licence suspended, or their right to obtain a licence suspended if they do not hold a licence.

This suspension is applied in accordance with the *Code of Penal Procedure* and remains in effect until the Société has been notified that the fine has been paid. The offender is prohibited from operating any vehicle for the duration of the suspension. Failure to respect this restriction could result in vehicle seizure and impoundment for 30 days.

DEMERIT POINTS

The Société enters demerit points on the record of drivers for certain offences under the *Highway Safety Code*, a traffic-related statute or bylaw. The following table lists offences and the corresponding number of demerit points.

OFFENCE	Number of points
For all licence holders:	
Speed in excess of the limit prescribed or indicated on a traffic control device	
• by 11 to 20 km/h	1
• by 21 to 30 km/h	2
• by 31 to 45 km/h	3
• by 46 to 60 km/h	5
• by 61 to 80 km/h	7
• by 81 to 100 km/h	9
• by 101 to 120 km/h	12
• by 121 km/h or more	15 or more

OFFENCE	Number of points
Accelerating when being overtaken	2
Failure to yield to pedestrians and cyclists at an intersection	2
Failure to yield to oncoming traffic	2
Passing a bicycle too closely in a lane of traffic	2
Tailgating	2
Sudden unnecessary braking	2
Travelling too fast for weather or road conditions	2
Illegal passing on the right	3
Illegal passing on the left	3
Illegal crossing of a solid line to overtake a vehicle	3
Illegal backing up	3
Failure to stop before turning right at a red traffic light (where turning right at a red light is permitted)	3
Failure to come to a complete stop at a level crossing	3
Failure to obey a red traffic light or stop sign	3
Failure to obey the order or signal of a law enforcement officer, school crossing guard or flagperson	3
Failure to wear a helmet (motorcycles, mopeds & motorized scooters)	3
Failure to wear a seat belt	3
Illegal passing in a lane reserved for oncoming traffic	4

OFFENCE	Number of points
Zigzagging in and out of traffic to pass	4
Speeding or reckless driving	4
Driving for a wager or stake or in a race	6
Prohibited use of a tunnel by a vehicle carrying hazardous material	9
Failure of a driver involved in an accident to do his or her duty	9
Failure to stop when approaching a school bus with its flashing lights in operation OR illegal passing of such a vehicle in either direction	9
Failure to stop at a level crossing when driving a bus, minibus or heavy vehicle carrying certain categories of hazardous material OR setting such a vehicle in motion again when prohibited	9
For holders of a learner's licence, probationary licence or licence authorizing the operation of a vehicle equipped with an alcohol ignition interlock device; also for holders under age 25 of a licence for less than 5 years authorizing only the operation of a moped or of a farm tractor	
Driving with the presence of alcohol in the body	4
Driving without an accompanying rider (learner's licence holders only)	4
Failure to provide a breath sample	4

ACCUMULATION OF DEMERIT POINTS

A learner's licence or probationary licence holder who has accumulated 4 or more demerit points receives a notice from the Société informing the driver of licence suspension.

A driver's licence holder who has accumulated 7 or more demerit points receives a notice from the Société urging improved driving habits. An additional notice is sent each time new demerit points are added to that driver's record. When the number of points reaches 15, the licence is revoked or the right to a licence suspended, whether or not the holder receives notice.

A person whose driver's licence has been revoked must surrender the licence at the request of the Société within 10 days of the date the revocation takes effect, failing which he or she becomes liable to a fine of $300 to $600.

Heavy vehicle drivers covered by the *Act respecting owners and operators of heavy vehicles*, and drivers of a taxi or emergency vehicle are required to inform the person responsible for the vehicle, or the owner of the taxi or emergency vehicle, when their driver's licence (or class of licence) has been modified, suspended or revoked.

LENGTH OF PENALTY

A person whose driver's licence has been revoked or the right to obtain one suspended due to an accumulation of demerit points can obtain a new driver's licence only after a period of time set by the *Highway Safety Code*. Time periods vary according to type of licence and point limits.

4 DEMERIT POINTS

For new drivers:

- a person who holds a class 5 or 6A learner's licence and who does not yet hold a driver's licence;

- a person who holds a probationary licence;
- a person who holds a class 6D licence (moped or scooter) or a class 8 licence (farm tractor), under age 25 and who has held the licence for less than 5 years.

The Code prescribes a 3 month licence suspension where the driver accumulates 4 points or more in his file. Since probationary licence holders under age 25 must have 2 years' experience driving with a valid licence, the length of their probation period will be extended an additional period equivalent to the suspension period. When they are again eligible for a licence, they must go to a Société service centre to reinstate their licence and driving privilege.

15 DEMERIT POINTS

A licence is revoked or the right to obtain a licence suspended for a period of 3, 6 or 12 months, depending on whether the driver has accumulated 15 demerit points for the first, second or third time in the previous 2 years.

To obtain a new driver's licence, the person must schedule an appointment to take a knowledge test when he/she is again eligible to hold a licence and pay applicable test and licence fees. It should be noted that the cost of a new licence will be increased by a higher insurance premium under the public plan, which is established on the basis of a driver's demerit points.

POINTS WRITTEN OFF

Demerit points remain on a driver's record for 2 years after the conviction that brought about their entry on the driving record, or payment of the fine (payment of a fine is equivalent to a conviction).

When a licence has become subject to a penalty resulting from the accumulation of demerit points, 4 or 15 points are written off the offending driver's record, depending on the type of licence. However, any demerit points that exceed these numbers will remain on the record for 2 years.

For example, for a licence holder who has accumulated 14 demerit points, a subsequent offence will bring that number to 16. Since the 15 point level has been reached, the driver's licence is revoked and 15 points are erased. The remaining demerit point stays on the driver's record for 2 years following the latest conviction.

No points are written off upon renewal of a driver's or learner's licence, nor upon the issue of a first licence, or of a new licence following revocation.

DEMERIT POINTS AND A RESTRICTED LICENCE

A driver whose licence has been suspended or revoked as a result of a first-time accumulation of demerit points in 2 years (4 points for probationary licence, or 15 demerit points for a driver's licence) may obtain a restricted licence where his/her livelihood requires the operation of a motor vehicle. To obtain a restricted licence, the person must apply to a Court of Québec judge for a restricted licence and notify the Société of the application. The applicant has to prove that driving is an essential aspect of his/her work and petition the judge to obtain the order authorizing him/her to hold a restricted licence.

Upon presentation of this order, the Société will issue a restricted licence.

CRIMINAL CODE OFFENCES

A person convicted of any of the following *Criminal Code* offences will see his/her licence revoked or the right to obtain a licence suspended:

- Criminal negligence of a motor vehicle causing death or bodily harm;
- Manslaughter resulting from the operation of a motor vehicle;
- Dangerous driving (in light of weather, road and traffic conditions at the time or reasonably expected use of vehicle);
- Dangerous driving causing death or bodily harm;
- Refusal to stop during a police pursuit;
- Leaving the scene of an accident;
- Refusal to submit to a breathalyzer test or to provide a blood sample;
- Driving or charge of a vehicle while impaired by alcohol or drugs and causing death or bodily harm;
- Driving or having care of a vehicle while impaired by alcohol or drugs and causing death or bodily harm;
- Driving or having care of a vehicle while one's blood alcohol level is over .08% (80 mg of alcohol per 100 ml of blood).

The Société is notified of driving-related criminal offences committed in another Canadian province or equivalent offences in a U.S. state with which Québec has a reciprocal agreement. Such offences are entered on the driver's record and result in the same penalty as if the offence took place in Québec.

PENALTIES FOR ALCOHOL-IMPAIRED DRIVING

Measures adopted to counter alcohol-impaired driving are based on prevention, that is, the identification and monitoring of persons who have difficulty disassociating alcohol consumption with driving a vehicle. Measures are more severe for repeat offenders in an effort to persuade them to change their behaviour regarding alcohol consumption.

Zero alcohol rule

Under the *Highway Safety Code*, the following persons cannot drive, or have the care or control of a motor vehicle if there is the presence of alcohol in their body:

- a person who does not hold a licence and who has never held a driver's licence other than that which authorizes driving only a moped, scooter (class 6D) or farm tractor (class 8);

- a person who holds a learner's licence which authorizes driving a passenger vehicle (class 5) or motorcycle (class 6A), unless he/she has previously held a driver's licence for a class of vehicle other than 6D or 8;

- a person who holds a probationary licence;

- a person who holds a driver's licence authorizing only the driving of a moped, scooter (class 6D) or farm tractor (class 8), under age 25 and who has held a licence for less than 5 years;

- a person who holds a restricted licence issued following the suspension of a probationary licence;

- a person who holds a licence authorizing only the driving of a vehicle equipped with an alcohol ignition interlock device;

- a person who holds a licence requiring that he/she must maintain a zero blood alcohol level to drive, or have the care or control of a motor vehicle.

IMMEDIATE LICENCE SUSPENSION

A law enforcement officer immediately suspends the licence or right to obtain a licence for a 30-day period:

1. of any person subject to the zero alcohol rule who drives, or has the care or control of a motor vehicle and has the presence of alcohol in his/her body;

2. of any person who drives, or has the care or control of a motor vehicle when his/her blood alcohol level is over .08;

3. of any person who refuses to provide a breath or blood sample.

The suspension period imposed by the law enforcement officer is 90 days if the person has had a previous conviction of an impaired driving offence within the last 10 years.

LENGTH OF DRIVING PROHIBITION

When a driver is convicted of an offence under the *Criminal Code*, a judge can impose a driving prohibition period. The period varies according to the offender's driving record and the type of offence.

A fine of $600 to $2000 may accompany a driving prohibition period in the case of a first offence; fines for subsequent offences are at the discretion of the judge. The offender may also be subject to a prison term.

The *Highway Safety Code* provides for revocation of a learner's licence, probationary licence or driver's licence as well as suspension of the right to obtain one of these licences. The minimum period of licence revocation or suspension of the right to obtain a licence is 1, 3 or 5 years, depending on the number of times the offender's licence has been revoked or suspended in the previous 10 years for an alcohol-related driving conviction.

If a court imposes a driving prohibition period longer than the revocation period provided in the *Highway Safety Code*, the judge's decision prevails and the driving prohibition period shall apply.

CONDITIONS FOR REINSTATING A LICENCE

A person whose licence has been revoked following a criminal conviction for impaired driving is required to meet particular conditions before a licence can be reinstated. The *Highway Safety Code* provides that:

- for a **first offence** within the last 10 years:
  - the offender must successfully complete the **Alcofrein** driver education program recognized by the Minister of Public Security that is intended to raise awareness about drinking and driving problems and prevent a repeat offence;
  - the offender must undergo a **summary assessment** conducted by a duly authorized person who works in an addiction rehabilitation centre. The final assessment report must show that the offender's behaviour is consistent with the safe operation of a vehicle.

If the results of the assessment are favourable, the offender may obtain a licence at the end of the revocation period.

If, however, the results of the assessment are unfavourable, the offender must undergo a **comprehensive assessment** (the same procedure applies to a repeat offender). Furthermore, once this process has been completed and the offender would like to obtain a new licence, for a period of **1 year** he/she will only be allowed to drive a vehicle equipped with an **alcohol ignition interlock**;

- **for a repeat offence** within 10 years:
  - the offender must undergo a **comprehensive assessment** over a period of 7 to 9 months, the purpose of which is to render his/her relationship to alcohol consistent with the safe operation of a vehicle. Before a new licence can be issued, this assessment should clearly demonstrate, to the satisfaction of the Société, that his/her alcohol consumption habits do not compromise the safe operation of a motor vehicle. The assessment must be conducted by a duly authorized person who works in an addiction rehabilitation centre or service;
  - the mandatory installation of an alcohol ignition interlock device is required for a period of 2 years for a second conviction or 3 years for a third conviction or more.

Fees to register in the Alcofrein program and the costs of summary and comprehensive assessments must be assumed by participants.

LICENCE REQUIRING USE OF AN ALCOHOL IGNITION INTERLOCK DEVICE

After the driving prohibition period handed down by the court, the driver **may** apply to the Société for a restricted licence, which will be valid until the end of the driver's licence revocation period imposed under the *Highway Safety Code*. An offender may also apply for a restricted licence during the driving prohibition period, subject to a court authorization. A restricted licence authorizes the offender to drive a vehicle on the condition that it is equipped with an alcohol ignition interlock device. This device prevents engine operation if it detects the presence of alcohol in the driver's body.

At the end of the licence revocation period, use of an alcohol ignition interlock device is **mandatory** in order to obtain a new licence in the following cases:

- if the driver is a repeat offender (2 or 3-year mandatory use);
- if the summary assessment is unfavourable for a first-time offending driver (mandatory use for 1 year).

If the offending driver wishes to drive at the end of the penalty period and if he/she has not received a satisfactory assessment report, the applicant **may** obtain, on a **voluntary** basis, a licence authorizing him/her to drive only a vehicle equipped with an alcohol ignition interlock. However, the period during which he/she drives using the device will not reduce the period of mandatory use imposed.

To obtain a licence authorizing driving with an alcohol ignition interlock, the driver must also meet the following conditions:

- have no other penalty on his/her record;
- submit proof of an agreement to install an ignition interlock device by a Société-approved shop;
- observe the terms of use for the interlock device;
- assume costs relating to use of the device.

A licence requiring use of an ignition interlock device cannot be issued for motorcycle classes or for a learner.

The licence classes authorized are those held by the driver at the time the penalty was imposed.

If the supplier of an ignition interlock device informs the Société that a driver is not complying with operating conditions, the Société may revoke or suspend the licence.

VEHICLE SEIZURE

A vehicle can be seized, towed immediately and impounded for 30 days, whether or not the offending driver is the vehicle owner if:

- the driver's licence has been revoked or suspended due to a *Criminal Code* offence, an accumulation of demerit points, an unpaid fine or for medical reasons;

- a motor vehicle is not equipped with an ignition interlock device, despite the fact that the driver's licence authorizes him/her to drive only a vehicle fitted with this device;

- the driver fails to respect ignition interlock conditions or drives with the presence of alcohol in the body;

- the driver fails to respect the terms of a restricted licence issued because of demerit points;

- the driver does not hold a valid driver's licence, of a class appropriate for the type of vehicle used and carrying the mandatory endorsements (in the case of heavy vehicles);

- the holder of a learner's licence for a motorcycle (6R) is operating the vehicle outside of a driving school's course or a road test for the SAAQ.

If the driver is not the owner of the motor vehicle, he/she is required to immediately notify the vehicle owner of its seizure. The driver is also responsible for submitting to the vehicle owner a copy of the seizure report.

In order to recover the vehicle, the owner must pay all towing and storage charges, and then take the appropriate steps for reimbursement by the offender.

FINES FOR DRIVING DURING A PENALTY PERIOD

A person who drives a vehicle while his/her licence is subject to a penalty must, in addition to dealing with an immediate seizure, pay a fine generally between $300 and $600. If a penalty period had been imposed for impaired driving, the fine will be $1,500 to $3,000.

An owner who allows use of a vehicle by someone whose licence has been suspended or revoked is liable to a fine of $300 to $600; if the person's licence had been revoked for impaired driving, the owner's fine will be $1,500 to $3,000.

Before lending or renting out a vehicle, the owner can check the validity of the driver's licence with the Société by calling 1 900 565-1212. There is a charge of $1.50 per call for the automated service.

The table below lists the statutes and penalties imposed under the *Criminal Code* and *Highway Safety Code* following a conviction for impaired driving:

	Criminal Code	Highway Safety Code

1st penalty	• Driver prohibited from driving for 1 year
	• Possible use of an ignition interlock device if authorized by a judge subsequent to a minimum 3-month driving prohibition period
	• Minimum fine of $600
		• Licence revoked for 1 year
		• Mandatory Alcofrein program
		• Summary assessment of behaviour regarding alcohol inconsistent with safe operation of a vehicle
		• If summary assessment unfavorable:
		  - comprehensive assessment
		  - mandatory ignition interlock for 1 year after revocation and once the evaluation meets Société recommendations

2nd penalty	• Driver prohibited from driving for 2 years • Possible use of an ignition interlock device if authorized by judge subsequent to a minimum 6-month driving prohibition period • Minimum 14-day prison term	• Licence revoked for 3 years • Comprehensive assessment • Mandatory ignition interlock for 2 years after revocation and once the evaluation meets Société recommendations
3rd or subsequent penalty	• Driver prohibited from driving for 3 years • Possible use of an ignition interlock device if authorized by judge subsequent to a minimum 12-month driving prohibition period • Minimum 90-day prison term	• Licence revoked for 5 years • Comprehensive assessment Mandatory ignition interlock for 3 years after revocation and once the evaluation meets Société recommendations
Reference period for calculating subsequent offence	• 10 years	
Other provisions		• Immediate 30- to 90-day licence suspension for alcohol and driving without an ignition interlock device • Zero alcohol for new drivers • Vehicle seizure for driving during penalty period or without a licence: 30 days • $1,500 to $3,000 fine if alcohol-related penalty

NB Under the *Criminal Code*, following a conviction for impaired driving causing bodily harm, the maximum prison term is 10 years. A conviction for impaired driving causing death may result in a term of life imprisonment.

RIGHT OF CHALLENGE

An individual whose licence or right to obtain one has been suspended for 90 days following a repeat impaired driving offence may file an application with the Société for a review of the suspension but he/she must assume the related costs. If a suspension is lifted, the Société reimburses costs incurred by the applicant. If the suspension is maintained following a review, the applicant may, within 10 days, contest the decision before the Administrative Tribunal of Québec.

The *Highway Safety Code* makes provisions for other circumstances which give an individual the right to contest certain decisions of the Société before the Administrative Tribunal of Québec, within 60 days of the decision. A person may appeal to the Tribunal when the Société has refused to issue or renew his/her driver's licence, probationary licence or learner's licence, or suspended it on medical grounds or for failure to submit the required medical examination or health assessment report.

A vehicle owner may petition the Court of Québec or apply to the Société for the lifting of a vehicle seizure.

The Société may review a decision at any time unless it has been challenged before the Tribunal or a court.

FACTORS THAT INFLUENCE DRIVING

At first glance, a driver's task appears rather straightforward. Driving, however, requires more than simply starting the engine, steering and bringing the vehicle to a stop. A driver has to master driving techniques and traffic rules and understand that the decisions he/she makes must take into account other drivers as well as road and traffic conditions.

Statistics on accidents and traffic offences, not to mention the number of victim's injured or killed each year on the road, bear witness to the complexity of the task.

Driving a vehicle calls on a driver's knowledge and the information he/she picks up while driving. A driver must therefore know how to interpret his/her surroundings, and be prepared to react and anticipate the reactions of others and before making a decision. A driver's decisions reflect his/her assessment of a situation. On approaching an intersection, for example, there is more involved than simply recognizing a stop sign and stopping. The driver has to assess the distance between the vehicle and the stop sign based on his/her speed, the road conditions and the presence of others on the road to determine the rate at which the vehicle must slow and where it will come to a stop.

New and experienced drivers will acknowledge that health, personality and surroundings are often factors that play a role in their driving. A driver's decisions are influenced by dominant character traits, mood and general well-being.

A motor vehicle operator's physical and psychological state are crucial to safe use of the roadway.

VISION

Safe operation of a vehicle depends on eyesight. Studies have shown that 90% of a driver's decisions are based on information gathered through the eye. Loss of visual acuity or field of vision has an immediate affect on performance, primarily at the time a decision must be made on the roadway. Therein lies the risk of an accident, both for the operator and other road users.

A number of elements come into play in giving the driver an accurate picture of his/her surroundings. Impairment of one aspect, especially if the driver is unaware of the weakness, can be dangerous and may even render the person unfit to drive.

VISUAL ACUITY

Visual acuity is the ability to clearly distinguish objects from a distance. Acuity varies from one individual to another and those with a below-average ability to see things sharply may not be aware of many details they are missing; they think they can see as well as others. A loss of visual acuity is generally associated with aging and a person's health. Only periodic eye examinations will reveal a progressive deterioration of visual acuity.

FIELD OF VISION

The visual field is the expanse of space in which objects are perceived while the eyes focus on one particular point. The area of a driver's visual field must be large enough to view at a glance any obstacle in front or on either side of the vehicle. It is as important as good visual acuity since an impaired visual field increases the risk of accidents.

A driver's field of vision narrows as the speed of a vehicle increases. It is the same when the eye focuses on one object. Drugs, alcohol and fatigue often produce the same effect. An eye condition and neurological disorder may also seriously impair the field of vision. Even wide eyeglass rims can affect the field of vision.

STEREOSCOPIC VISION

Stereoscopic vision, or depth perception, is a person's ability to accurately situate objects in three-dimensional space. It enables a driver to estimate the distance between his/her vehicle and other objects around even when those objects are in motion.

CORRECTIVE LENSES

Contact lenses and eyeglasses should be worn if required. Someone with a driver's licence that bears the "A" condition must wear lenses or glasses for driving. Failure to comply is an offence punishable by a fine.

It is always more hazardous to drive at night than during the day, regardless of a driver's visual acuity. Adapting to night driving means reducing speed, given the limited scope of a vehicle's headlights.

Road signs are covered with a material that reflects a vehicle's headlight, allowing a driver to see them from farther away than other non-reflective objects. A driver therefore should not judge the reach of a vehicle's lights by the reflection from a sign.

Two factors are crucial to night driving:

- the driver's ability to see under little light;
- resistance to glare.

As a person ages, his/her ability to adjust to glare is reduced. If night driving is particularly difficult, greater caution is necessary.

Wearing tinted glasses is strongly discouraged at night; they inevitably reduce a driver's visual acuity.

PHYSICAL DISORDERS

Some physical ailments may be the direct cause of an accident. Health care professionals can report the name and address of any patient age 14 or older whom they deem unfit to drive on the basis of health or vision. A professional who makes such a report cannot be sued for damages.

By reason of a person's state of health, the Société may suspend or refuse to issue a licence, or change the conditions on a licence. It may also require the individual involved to submit to further examination or assessment by a health care professional. Obviously, a responsible driver will comply with the recommendations of his/her physician.

Temporary conditions such as headaches and fever make driving more difficult. A person should obviously not get behind the wheel if this is the case. A driver who feels ill while traveling should find a safe spot off the road to stop the vehicle.

FATIGUE

When we're tired, our ability to drive is diminished and the consequences could be disastrous.

Drowsiness has many causes. In some cases, it follows a heavy meal. Most often it is the result of a lack of sleep, the monotony of the road, lack of practice for night driving or the temperature inside a vehicle.

Drowsiness can affect alertness. A driver must consider the first signs of drowsiness a clear warning of the risk of an accident.

Because fatigue slows muscle coordination, a driver who feels tired, who yawns, whose eyes are irritated or who has short hallucinations must stop for awhile. Stretching the legs may be all that is needed. Sometimes a short nap may leave a driver feeling refreshed.

A person's mental or psychological state is also an important factor in the safe operation of a motor vehicle. An individual who is experiencing an extreme emotion such as anger or grief should therefore refrain from driving.

ALCOHOL

Impaired driving is a serious social concern! In Québec, alcohol use is a factor in about 31% of fatal accidents, 18% of accidents causing serious injury and 5% of accidents causing minor injury. In 2001, alcohol accounted for 190 deaths and 3,100 injured.

Alcohol compels a driver to take risks. Today, it is common knowledge that alcohol impairs a person's ability to drive. The more a person drinks, the poorer his/her ability to exercise safe judgment.

Driving under the influence of alcohol significantly increases the risk of a serious accident, with its dire consequences and increasingly harsher penalties.

Just one glass of wine may produce the effects described above. Even if a person's blood alcohol level is below .08% these effects may appear, since at .05% the faculties of an average adult are significantly affected. It is important to note that young drivers are more easily affected, and by smaller amounts of alcohol. **A driver aged 16 to 19 with a blood alcohol level of .03 is three times more at risk of becoming involved in a fatal accident.**

The effects of alcohol surface relatively quickly if a person is tired or drinks on an empty stomach. The more alcohol ingested, the more serious the impairment. No person should drive after drinking.

Since alcohol is consumed on a number of different occasions, it is important to reduce the impact of alcohol by exercising moderation and reminding guests at a reception of their responsibility.

Some recommendations:

- drink very little and slowly;
- have something to eat when drinking;
- serve non-alcoholic beverages (including water);
- space your drinks;
- stop serving alcohol at least an hour before the end of the reception;
- take steps to ensure that you do not operate a vehicle while impaired – have another person drive or take a taxi or bus;
- allow a guest who has had too much to drink to stay over.

Many people believe that a person who is used to drinking will be better able to "handle" alcohol and avoid being impaired. While it is true that the habitual drinker's body adjusts, the impression of sobriety is illusory, leading the person to overestimate his/her ability to drive.

Popular remedies for reducing the effects of alcohol rarely work. Some people believe that eating while drinking helps the elimination process. The presence of food in the stomach, however, merely slows down the absorption of alcohol into the blood; it does not prevent the person from reaching a higher blood alcohol concentration.

The fact remains that the liver breaks down 90% of alcohol consumed by an individual. A healthy individual's liver works at a steady rate, processing a given number of mg in an hour, regardless of the amount consumed. It takes at least 5 hours for the body to eliminate the amount of alcohol consumed by someone with a .08% blood alcohol concentration.

Taking a walk or shower will not speed up the alcohol elimination process. There is no miraculous method for increasing the body's ability to metabolize alcohol. Time is the only remedy.

MAIN EFFECTS OF ALCOHOL ON A VEHICLE OPERATOR

On observation

- Rather than scanning the road ahead, to the sides and occasionally behind, a driver under the influence of alcohol tends to focus on one spot or object ahead: he/she pays less attention to vehicles, persons and objects on or near the road.

- The driver is less able to estimate distances between objects.

- The driver is less able to adapt to darkness.

- At night, a driver has difficulty focusing after encountering the glare of an oncoming vehicle and the time it takes to adjust after the vehicle has passed is longer than normal.

- There is a decreased sense of danger and the driver therefore takes more risks.

On decision-making

- Brain activity is slowed.

- The driver is less able to recognize a problem situation.

- Making a quick decision is difficult.

On execution

- The stimulation provoked by alcohol results in overconfidence of one's abilities.

- Slower brain activity results in a loss of muscular coordination. Since a driver is slow to realize that he/she must act, limb movements are often abrupt and imprecise. He/she finds it difficult to stay in the lane, go through an intersection, change lanes, make a turn, control the vehicle and even come to a stop. Alcohol will also affect the sense of balance of a motorcycle rider.

DRUGS AND MEDICATION

It is common knowledge that drugs and some medications have an impact on an individual's ability to operate a motor vehicle. The use of drugs (marijuana, cocaine, amphetamines, etc.) or mood-altering medications (minor tranquilizers, anti-depressants, sedatives, etc.) increase the risk of accident. In combination with alcohol the risk climbs significantly.

PRECAUTIONS

A driver taking medication must make a reasonable assessment of whether its use is consistent with the safe operation of a vehicle.

Taken alone, some medications have effects similar to those produced by alcohol. This is particularly true for minor tranquilizers or sleeping pills.

Antihistamines (in the form of syrup or pills) to relieve allergy or cold symptoms can cause drowsiness. A person using such medication should read the label carefully and ask a physician or pharmacist about side effects and the likely impact on the ability to drive.

A driver under medication should never drink alcohol. Such a combination is dangerous because the side effects of the medication are multiplied by those of the alcohol. The combined effects significantly impair a person's ability to react and may leave him/her completely unable to drive.

A DRIVER'S MIND-SET

Although a driver's physical health is important, his/her mental health requires serious consideration. Personality traits often show up in behaviour at the controls of a motor vehicle, which provides an individual with a feeling of independence and serves as an outlet for emotions.

Some drivers show self-respect and consideration. In a difficult driving situation, their decisions are based on tolerance, patience and foresight. Fully aware of the inherent danger involved in operating a motor vehicle, their skills and driving habits improve with experience.

However, some situations are more likely to lead to conflicts between drivers, for example, city rush hours or getting on and off highways. People react in a wide variety of ways to traffic jams. To avoid making a bad situation worse, a driver must moderate his/her behaviour and anticipate possible danger.

Regardless of the cause of a traffic problem, it is sometimes best just to slow down and, if necessary, pull off to the side of the road. This does not mean being passive; it means being alert.

A good driver should plan ahead, choosing travel times and routes that make it possible to avoid traffic congestion and the likelihood of an accident. These are preferable alternatives to using the shoulder of the road or stop-and-go tactics to move forward faster than the person ahead.

OBSERVATION

Observing the immediate surroundings and checking on all sides of the vehicle are key to determining if one can safely overtake a vehicle, change lanes, proceed through an intersection or merge with traffic. A driver must base the decision to proceed or yield the way to other road users on information he or she receives through direct observation. A driver must also adjust his/her speed to traffic conditions.

We must think about what happens when a driver goes through an intersection without stopping and making the necessary verifications, or a driver who overtakes a vehicle without checking for oncoming traffic. Serious accidents and victims who had the misfortune of being in the wrong place at the wrong time are commonplace. Negligence increases the risk of accident.

EXERCISING JUDGMENT

A greater number of accidents occur at night and on weekends; vigilance is especially called for during these times. The possibility of human error is all around, in the vehicle ahead or behind, in the oncoming vehicle or the one overtaking you. Your judgment may be called upon at any moment.

Unexpected situations may call for reduced speed. Road building or repair work, a mishap, fog, etc., may test one's patience and leave little time for proper response.

All drivers will encounter situations that are beyond their control, for example a traffic light may be defective, the driver in front may appear lost or is driving too slowly or any other unexpected situation may cause a driver to lengthen or change his/her route.

This is when a driver must exercise judgment. Obviously, no one takes pleasure in yielding to or being intimidated by other drivers or backing down from a risky venture. A hurried action, however, can lead to a dramatic situation. Inconvenience or delay is the small price a smart driver is willing to pay for safer roads.

Chapter 2

THE VEHICLE

*A*ll road vehicles must be registered to be used on a public roadway in Québec. Owners are responsible for having their vehicle registered at a Société de l'assurance automobile du Québec service centre.

Owners must pay their registration fees every year so they can continue to drive their vehicle.

The *Highway Safety Code* and its regulations also require vehicle owners to maintain their vehicles properly and to ensure that they have the features and accessories required by law.

VEHICLE REGISTRATION

IN GENERAL

Every road vehicle must be registered unless exempted under the *Highway Safety Code*. The owner is responsible for applying to the Société de l'assurance automobile du Québec on taking possession of a vehicle or before expiry of temporary registration from a vehicle dealer. A vehicle owner who takes up residence in Québec must apply for registration within 90 days.

The registration remains valid for as long as the vehicle and the owner remain the same.

When the vehicle is registered, the Société issues a licence plate and registration certificate that corresponds to the owner category and vehicle type, use and place of operation.

VEHICLES EXEMPT FROM REGISTRATION

Registration is not required for the following road vehicles, which are not used on public roads:

- snowblowers with a net weight of 900 kg or less;
- farm tractors that are not used on public roads;
- snowmobiles with a net weight of 55 kg or less and a maximum speed under 15 km/h;
- snowmobiles, with a net weight of 450 kg or less that are owned by a person who does not reside in Québec provided that the snowmobile is registered in compliance with the laws of the owner's place of residence or head office;
- motorized toy vehicles that can carry one person;
- golf carts;
- garden tractors, not including farm tractors, and riding mowers that carry one person;
- road vehicles used exclusively inside a building;
- farm machinery owned by a farmer.

OBTAINING A VEHICLE'S REGISTRATION AND THE RIGHT TO OPERATE THE VEHICLE

REQUIREMENTS

To register a vehicle and obtain the right to operate it on the road, owners must:

- meet the terms and conditions set out by regulation;
- pay the fees set by regulation;
- following the purchase of a used vehicle, submit the odometer reading at the time of registration.

As well, their driver's licence must not be currently suspended for unpaid fines.

Owners of heavy vehicles (trucks or buses with a net weight of more than 3,000 kg) and owners of tow trucks or road vehicles used to transport hazardous material must enter their vehicles in the register of owners and operators of heavy vehicles kept by the Commission des Transports du Québec.

COST OF REGISTRATION

The cost of registration varies according to vehicle type, use and place of operation. It includes:

- the registration fee;
- the Québec automobile insurance plan premium;
- administrative charges;
- a contribution of motorists to public transit, if applicable;
- sales tax.

Additional charges are added for passenger vehicles that are no more than seven years old and valued at over $40,000.

MANDATORY LIABILITY INSURANCE

The *Automobile Insurance Act* requires every vehicle owner to have third-party liability insurance coverage in the amount of at least $50,000. This is a legal obligation for anyone who plans to drive on public roads in Québec.

SPECIAL REQUIREMENT FOR MINORS

Minors who wish to register a vehicle must provide the Société with written consent from their parent or legal guardian.

CASES IN WHICH VEHICLE REGISTRATION MAY BE DENIED

The Société will not register a vehicle if the applicant cannot prove sole or joint ownership, or prove that the vehicle is owned by a business in which he/she has an interest.

CONDITIONS RELATING TO VEHICLE REGISTRATION

SIGNATURE

The person in whose name a registration certificate is issued must sign it as soon as he/she receives it.

CHANGE OF ADDRESS

The person whose name appears on the registration certificate must inform the Société of any change of address within 30 days.

MOTOR VEHICLE LIABILITY INSURANCE CARD

A person who drives, has charge of or exercises control over a motor vehicle must carry the vehicle's registration certificate and vehicle liability insurance card and must be able to show them upon request by a law enforcement officer.

LICENCE PLATE INSTALLATION

Vehicle owners must securely attach their licence plates to the rear of their vehicles or elsewhere as determined by regulation.

However, owners of combination vehicles designed to pull a trailer must attach the licence plate to the front of the vehicle.

LEGIBLE AND CLEAN LICENCE PLATES

Only the inscription determined by the Société may appear on a licence plate.

The licence plate must be kept free of any matter that might prevent it from being clearly legible. There must also be sufficient lighting at the rear to make it visible at night.

A law enforcement officer may require that the operator of a motor vehicle clean the licence plate if it is so dirty that it is hard to read.

NO OTHER PLATES ALLOWED

No plate that might be confused with one issued by the Société or an equivalent authority in another jurisdiction may be affixed to a vehicle, unless another Québec statute so requires.

CERTIFICATE AND PLATE REPLACEMENT

The holder of a registration certificate that is damaged, illegible or lost must apply to the Société for a replacement. A fee will be charged for the new certificate.

Anyone who operates a vehicle with a licence plate that is so damaged that it is illegible is subject to a fine.

ANNUAL REGISTRATION FEES

To retain the right to drive their vehicles, owners have to pay registration fees every year no later than the due date set by regulation.

No grace period is allowed for late payment. The full amount indicated on the notice must be paid unless the vehicle owner is taking the vehicle off the road before the beginning of the new registration period. Additional charges are applied when registration fees are not paid before or by the deadline.

Owners who owe the Société an amount that has not been paid are not allowed to drive their vehicle.

DISCARDING A VEHICLE

Owners who discard a vehicle because it can no longer be used must inform the Société and declare that they will not be driving the vehicle anymore. These requests may be made by phone.

Before a discarded vehicle is authorized to be used once more on a public roadway, the owner must have the vehicle mechanically inspected, assuming all costs relating to such, and ensure that all repairs required to allow the vehicle to meet regulatory standards are met.

VEHICLE STORAGE

Vehicle owners who wish to store their vehicles for an indefinite amount of time must inform the Société. During this time, they cannot drive their vehicle but the licence plate must remain on it. The Société gives the vehicle owner a receipt to confirm that the vehicle is in storage. If the storage application is made by telephone, the owner is sent a letter to confirm the vehicle's change of status.

Reimbursement

If the vehicle is discarded, placed in storage, sold, damaged beyong repair, stolen or registered in another jurisdiction, the owner is entitled to be reimbursed for part of the amount paid to cover registration fees and the Québec automobile insurance plan premium.

CHANGE OF OWNERSHIP

When the ownership of a vehicle is transferred, supporting documents are required, for example a piece of identity, power of attorney where another person is being represented, or a document giving the parent's consent in the case of a minor. As well, no one whose driver's licence is suspended for unpaid fines may cede ownership of a vehicle.

Vehicle purchased from an individual

Before buying an individual's vehicle, the prospective purchaser should check with the SAAQ that an unpaid fine does not prevent a change of ownership.

When a vehicle is purchased from an individual, both the buyer and seller must go to the Société service centre. The person selling the vehicle must hand in the registration certificate. The vehicle is then issued a new registration confirming that the person acquiring the vehicle is the new owner.

Exchange of vehicles

When two people exchange road vehicles, each vehicle owner must apply for new registration and pay applicable fees.

Transaction through a dealer

A person who sells a road vehicle to a dealer must give the dealer the registration certificate, after having endorsed it.

If the person does not purchase a new vehicle, can he/she must turn in the licence plate to the Société.

If they do purchase a new vehicle, they must apply to the Société for its registration. The same licence plate can be used, if so desired.

RULES GOVERNING VEHICLES AND ACCESSORIES [2]

MANDATORY IDENTIFICATION NUMBERS

Road vehicles must bear manufacturers' serial numbers. The numbers manufacturers assign are recorded by the Société de l'assurance automobile du Québec. The Société may also assign and affix an identification number.

Vehicle owners who find that their vehicle does not show a serial number must apply to the Société to have one.

Changing, making illegible, defacing, removing and replacing a vehicle's serial number is prohibited without prior consent from the Société.

COMPULSORY EQUIPMENT AND ACCESSORIES

All road vehicles must include the features and accessories that the manufacturer is required to include under Québec statutes and regulations.

---

2. Farm-use vehicles are subject to specific traffic rules and safety standards.

Buses and minibuses used to carry school children must be equipped with signs at the front and rear that read "ÉCOLIERS" (school children).

If school children are carried in a passenger vehicle, the owner must install one of these signs on the vehicle roof, facing the front and back of the vehicle. These signs must be removed or covered up when the vehicle is not being used to carry school children.

LIGHTS AND SIGNALS

Drivers must make sure that the lights and signals required for their type of vehicle are in good working order and that they have not been soiled or obstructed in such a way as to make them less effective.

ROAD VEHICLES

All vehicles other than a motorcycle, moped or scooter travelling on public roadways must be equipped at the front with at least two single or twin white headlights, two white or amber parking lights, and two white or amber turn-signal lights.

At the rear, all vehicles, other than a motorcycle, moped or scooter, including trailers and semi-trailers, must have two red parking lights, two red reflectors (which may be part of the lens), two red brake lights, two red or amber turn-signal lights, a white backup light, and a white licence plate light. They must also have a red parking light and side-marker light at the rear and an amber parking light and side-marker light at the front on either side.

In addition, all vehicles that are 9.1 meters long or more must be equipped with an amber parking light and side-marker light on either side, halfway between the front and rear side-marker lights.

SPECIAL RULES FOR VEHICLES OVER 2.03 METRES WIDE

In addition to the lights required above, road vehicles and combination road vehicles that are over 2.03 metres wide must have an amber clearance light on each side and three amber parking lights in front, and a red clearance light on each side and three red parking lights at the rear.

MOTORCYCLES, MOPEDS AND SCOOTERS

Motorcycles, mopeds and scooters must be equipped with at least one white headlight, one red light at the rear, two white or yellow turn-signal lights at the front, two red or yellow turn-signal lights at the rear and one red brake light at the rear.

BUSES

Buses and minibuses used to carry school children must be equipped with flashing red lights at the front and rear, as well as a mandatory stop signal consisting of a retractable stop sign or retractable arm with a stop sign (ARRÊT). This signal must be installed on the outside near the driver's seat. These signals and lights must be used while children are boarding or leaving the bus.

FLASHING AND ROTATING LIGHTS

Rotating and flashing lights are reserved for certain types of vehicles. Red flashing or rotating lights are reserved for emergency vehicles, blue ones for police vehicles, and amber ones for service, equipment, escort, snow removal and road maintenance vehicles. Green flashing and rotating lights are reserved for emergency vehicles at disaster sites or for indicating a command post.

Fog lights

Optional fog lights must meet prescribed standards and be placed at the front of the vehicle at the same level – never higher – than headlights.

BRAKES

Road vehicles and combination road vehicles must be equipped with at least one service brake system that is in good working order and capable of applying sufficient braking power to each load-bearing wheel to stop the vehicle quickly in case of emergency, as well as parking brakes that keep it at a full stop.

It is an offence to drive a vehicle on which the brake system has been modified or altered in such a way as to reduce its effectiveness.

A law enforcement officer who has reasonable grounds to believe that the brake system of a road vehicle is defective or out of order may have the vehicle impounded or towed to the nearest suitable place for storage at the owner's expense until the situation has been rectified.

ALTERATION OF SEAT BELTS

Removal or alteration of a vehicle's seat belts is prohibited, as is having them rendered unusable. A fine of $200 may be imposed for such offences.

AIR BAG

Deactivation of an air bag installed in a motor vehicle is prohibited, except by means of a unit installed by the vehicle manufacturer prior to sale to the initial owner. Where an air bag requires replacement (due to deployment or damage) only new original manufacturer parts may be used. Failing this, a fine of $300 to $600 may be imposed.

RADAR WARNING DEVICES

The installation or sale of a radar warning device for a vehicle is prohibited.

Driving a vehicle equipped with such a device is forbidden. A law enforcement officer who has reasonable grounds to believe that a vehicle is equipped with a radar warning device may stop the vehicle for an inspection. If a device is found, the officer is authorized to confiscate it at the owner's expense, giving the driver a receipt. The device is then turned over to the Société de l'assurance automobile du Québec, which may dispose of it after 90 days.

HORNS

All vehicles must be equipped with a horn, which should only be used when necessary.

Only emergency vehicles may be equipped with sirens or devices that produce a similar warning sound or with mechanisms for changing traffic lights.

Under the *Highway Safety Code*, law enforcement officers may have an unauthorized siren or similar warning device removed from a vehicle at the owner's expense. The officer gives the driver a receipt before handing the siren or device over to the Société.

This rule does not apply to anti-theft devices installed on vehicles.

EXHAUST SYSTEM

A vehicle's exhaust system must include all its components, such as the manifold, pipes, muffler, supports and fasteners. These parts must all be securely fastened and none of them should have any gas leaks.

The sale of a vehicle with a sub-standard exhaust system for use on a public roadway is prohibited.

Modifying an exhaust system in such a way as to make it noisier, suppress it or reduce its effectiveness is also prohibited.

WINDSHIELDS AND WINDOWS

Vehicle windshields and windows must be made of transparent glass and manufactured or treated in such a way as to significantly reduce their risk of shattering or being broken. They must be kept free of foreign matter that might hamper the driver's view.

No substance that hinders visibility or darkens the glass may be applied to or sprayed on the windshield. A strip no more than 15 cm wide may, however, be placed along the upper edge of the windshield. Side windows on either side of the driver must let in at least 70% of the light when measured with a photometer.

A law enforcement officer may require a driver to clean or clear the windshield or windows of any foreign matter.

REARVIEW MIRRORS

All motor vehicles, except for motorcycles, mopeds and scooters, must have at least two securely attached rearview mirrors: one inside, in the centre of the upper part of the windshield, and one outside the driver's side.

When use of the inside mirror is impossible, an outside mirror similar to that on the driver's side must be attached to the right side of the vehicle.

Motorcycles, mopeds and motorized scooters must be equipped with a securely attached rearview mirror on each side.

SPEEDOMETER AND ODOMETER

All motor vehicles (except mopeds, scooters and motorcycles with an engine size up to 125 cc) must be equipped with a speedometer and odometer in good working order.

BUMPERS

Motor vehicle bumpers must be securely fixed in their intended location.

TIRES

Owners must ensure that their vehicles are equipped with tires that meet established standards for use on public roadways and that they are in good condition.

Studded tires may be used between October 15 and May 1 on passenger vehicles and commercial vehicles with a gross vehicle weight of 3,000 kg or less.

FENDERS

Motor vehicles or combination vehicles that are not equipped with permanent fenders must be fitted with mobile mudguards made of resistant material, and be no narrower than the tire tread. Farm tractors and machinery are exempt from this requirement.

NATURAL GAS AND PROPANE VEHICLES

Natural gas or propane vehicles must carry a compliance sticker certifying that the vehicle's fuel system meets the requirements of the *Regulation respecting safety standards for road vehicles*, failing which the vehicle owner is liable to a $300 to $600 fine.

MODIFYING A VEHICLE

Except with prior authorization by the Société de l'assurance automobile du Québec, no one may alter the frame, body or mechanisms of a vehicle intended for use on a public roadway if the alteration might decrease vehicle stability or braking effectiveness.

The Société's approval is also required before making an alteration that would change the vehicle type.

MECHANICAL INSPECTION

The Société de l'assurance automobile du Québec has exclusive authority over mechanical inspection of road vehicles and the issue of inspection certificates and compliance stickers.

Every year, the Société inspects thousands of vehicles stopped by law enforcement officers.

Accredited agents located throughout Québec carry out mechanical inspections. Agents are businesses accredited by the Société to carry out inspections of light vehicles (3,000 kg and less) or heavy vehicles (more than 3,000 kg), for a fee.

A law enforcement officer may require a mechanical inspection if there are reasonable grounds to believe that a vehicle has been modified or constitutes a public danger. He/she may also impound a vehicle at the owner's expense, so that an inspection can be carried out.

COMPULSORY INSPECTION

The following vehicles must be inspected:

- vehicles used by a driving school for teaching purposes;

- emergency vehicles;

- tow trucks that have a net weight of 3,000 kg or less;

- taxicabs, buses, minibuses and other vehicles used to carry school children;

- vehicles altered to use fuel other than that intended by the manufacturer;

- vehicles with a net weight over 3,000 kg, with the exception of motor homes, campers, tool vehicles, farm tractors, farm machinery, construction site trailers and farm trailers;

- modified, home-made or recycled vehicles, as well as any other vehicle that a law enforcement officer considers a public danger;

- vehicles involved in an accident;

- used vehicles originating outside Québec;

- vehicles that have been discarded.

A law enforcement officer may also order a mechanical inspection and set the deadline for the inspection if he/she has reasonable grounds to believe that a vehicle has undergone changes or is in a condition that constitutes a danger.

INSPECTION OUTCOME

If the vehicle meets regulatory standards, the Société or its agent issues a certificate of mechanical inspection and a compliance sticker.

Where minor repairs are needed, the owner or driver is given 48 hours to correct the situation, failing which the notice becomes a ticket and the vehicle is ordered off the road.

A vehicle that requires major repairs cannot be used on the road until it is shown to meet regulatory standards.

Furthermore, an owner who refuses or fails to submit a vehicle for mechanical inspection or who refuses to produce a certificate of mechanical inspection will not be allowed to drive the vehicle.

YOUR OWN INSPECTION

The vehicle equipment and features required for safe driving must be constantly kept in good working order.

Taking note of any odd sounds or other problems with your vehicle is a simple way of saving time and money and avoiding major headaches later. When carrying out your regular inspections, pay special attention to the following items:

BRAKES

Do your brakes squeak? Does your brake pedal respond immediately to pressure? Can you hear metal surfaces rubbing together? Does your vehicle pull to the left or right when you brake, or stop slowly even when you press down hard on the brake pedal?

HANDBRAKE

Does it hold your vehicle stationary when you are starting the engine or on a grade?

REARVIEW MIRRORS

Are both of the rearview mirrors securely attached? Are they cracked, chipped or tarnished so that they adversely affect visibility?

Are your mirrors adjusted properly, so that you can see well?

STEERING

Is there uneven wear on the tires? Have you noticed too much play in the steering – a definite tendency for the vehicle to pull to the right or left? Have you had any trouble controlling the vehicle? All these things are signs that your steering system should be checked and carefully adjusted. Have your wheel alignment checked at least once a year, and any time you think it might have been jolted out of line.

WINDSHIELD

What is the condition of your windshield wipers and your washer fluid distributor? Do they guarantee clear visibility at all times? Did you know that defective windshield wipers can damage your windshield?

TIRES

Check your tires regularly. Is there uneven or abnormal tire wear? Could this be caused by improper air pressure, infrequent tire rotation, poor alignment or wheel balance, or simply poor driving habits?

EXHAUST SYSTEM

Have you noticed any leaks in your muffler or exhaust system? You can usually hear them: louder-than-usual engine noise often indicates a problem with the exhaust system.

LIGHTS AND HEADLIGHTS

Are all lights in good condition and free of foreign matter?

SEAT BELT

Have you examined your seat belt for any cuts or tears in the fabric? Are the belt buckle and locking and unlocking mechanism present and in good working order?

HEADREST

If your vehicle is equipped with a headrest by the manufacturer, is the headrest still installed and in good condition? Is the middle of the headrest at eye level or level with the top of your ears? Is it near your head, i.e. no further away than 10 cm?

DRIVE BELTS

Did you know that the condition of your drive belts can be important to your safety? If the belt gives way suddenly in a vehicle with power steering, it will be difficult and even dangerous to drive.

Is the tension right? Check to make sure that belts are not cracked and that the fabric is not frayed or torn.

SHOCK ABSORBERS

Does your vehicle rock after going over a bump or coming out of a pothole? Is it sensitive to side-winds? Maybe your shock absorbers are not up to par.

To check them, push down hard on one corner of your vehicle and release. If the corner bounces more than once before resuming its initial position, the shock is probably faulty. Repeat for each corner of the vehicle.

BODY CONDITION

Are all the parts securely attached and in good working order? Pay special attention to holes in the floor, especially in the trunk, where highly toxic exhaust fumes might seep in.

Chapter 3
ROAD SIGNS AND TRAFFIC SIGNALS

*U*nder the *Highway Safety Code, road signs and traffic signals must meet the standards set by Transport Québec. These signs and signals are designed to ensure road users' safety and facilitate the flow of traffic.*

While useful as guides, signs and traffic signals cannot be construed as guarantees against the risks inherent in road use. Roadways, vehicles and rules are mainly developed under ideal traffic conditions. Because accident risks, when in traffic, are numerous, drivers must continually adjust their conduct.

Québec road signs and traffic signals include road signs, traffic lights and road markings. The signs form a visual language that vehicle operators must know and understand for their own safety and for the safety of other road users.

SIGNAL LIGHTS

Signal lights include all the lights that guide drivers and pedestrians on the roads. Apart from standard traffic lights, there are flashing lights, pedestrian lights, lights for cyclists, lane use lights, railway crossing lights, parking regulation lights, work site lights, priority lights for buses, as well as inspection station lights.

SIGNAL LIGHTS

TRAFFIC LIGHTS

Traffic lights are generally located at intersections; their purpose is to control the right of way of vehicles and pedestrians based on the flow of traffic. When lights are not working properly or at all, drivers must conduct themselves as if the intersection was controlled by mandatory stop signs for all directions, unless instructed otherwise by a road sign.

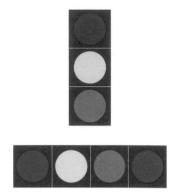

RED LIGHT

A red light means you must stop. Motor vehicle operators and cyclists must bring their vehicle to a full stop at the intersection, before coming to any marked pedestrian crosswalk or stop line. If there is no line, operators must stop before the edge of the roadway they are preparing to cross. The motorist or cyclist may only proceed on the authorization of a traffic signal. If there are no pedestrian lights, pedestrians must also stop.

YELLOW (AMBER) LIGHT

A yellow light indicates to motor vehicle operators and cyclists that they must stop before the pedestrian crosswalk or stop line. If there is no line, they must stop before the edge of the roadway they are preparing to cross, unless they are already in the intersection or are so close to it that the vehicle cannot be stopped safely. The motorist or cyclist may only proceed on the authorization of a traffic signal. If there are no pedestrian lights, pedestrians must follow the same rules.

SIGNAL LIGHTS

GREEN LIGHT

Motor vehicle operators and cyclists facing a solid or flashing green light may continue on their way after yielding the right of way to vehicles, cyclists or pedestrians already in the intersection. Pedestrians facing a green traffic light may cross the roadway if there are no pedestrian lights.

A flashing green light means that vehicles are given priority for a left turn by advancing the green while oncoming vehicles still face red.

RED ARROW

A red arrow prohibits drivers from going in the direction to which it points.

YELLOW ARROW

A yellow arrow has the same function as the amber light, but shows the direction of traffic.

GREEN ARROWS

A green arrow, whether flashing or not, indicates to motor vehicle operators or cyclists that they must proceed in the direction indicated, following the same rules for the right of way as those for a green light.

SIGNAL LIGHTS

FLASHING LIGHTS

Flashing yellow or red lights are used as additional signals to indicate a particularly dangerous intersection.

FLASHING RED LIGHT

Motor vehicle operators and cyclists approaching a flashing red light must come to a stop, yield the right of way to any vehicle on the intersecting roadway already in the intersection or near enough to it that to proceed might cause an accident. A flashing red light has the same function as the stop sign.

FLASHING YELLOW LIGHT

A flashing yellow light means that motor vehicle operators and cyclists must slow down and proceed with caution after yielding the right of way to other vehicles and pedestrians already in the intersection.

A flashing yellow light accompanying prescriptive or warning signs is used to direct attention to danger or obligation.

PEDESTRIAN LIGHTS

Pedestrian lights regulate pedestrian movement and help them avoid conflicts with road vehicles.

Standard lights show the outline of a walking person or an orange hand, while some lights show how much time is left before the hand appears.

PEDESTRIAN SILHOUETTE

Pedestrians facing this signal may proceed across the roadway in the area reserved for crossing. At certain intersections, an audio signal for the visually impaired will sound continuously while the silhouette is lit. When the symbol starts flashing, pedestrians already in the intersection must hurry to reach the sidewalk or median.

ORANGE HAND SILHOUETTE

Pedestrians facing this signal should not enter the intersection. When the signal begins to flash, pedestrians already in the intersection must be quick to reach the sidewalk or median.

TIME COUNTER

Some pedestrian lights count down the time remaining to cross in seconds.

CYCLIST LIGHTS

Cyclist lights, used to regulate bicycle traffic, are made up of three vertical lights in the form of red, yellow and green bicycles. The colours have the same meaning as traffic lights.

SIGNAL LIGHTS

LANE USE LIGHTS

Lane use lights consist of red lights in the shape of an X, green lights in the shape of an arrow pointed down and yellow flashing lights in the shape of a horizontal arrow. These lights are mounted over one or several lanes to indicate whether vehicle traffic is permitted or prohibited in the lanes. The meaning of the symbols is as follows:

RED X

Operators may not drive or stop in the lane under this signal.

GREEN ARROW POINTING DOWN

Operators may use the lane under this signal.

YELLOW HORIZONTAL ARROW

Usually appears in combination with the red X; it indicates that operators must, with caution, change lanes either to the left or right because of lane closure ahead.

RAILWAY CROSSING SIGNALS

These warning devices, consisting of flashing red lights, are placed at roadway-railway intersections. They indicate to drivers and pedestrians that a train is coming and that they must stop before the level crossing.

REGULATED PARKING LIGHTS

Regulated parking lights are made up of orange lights accompanied by a regulatory sign. These signs prohibit parking on the road at certain times to facilitate road maintenance. The prohibition on the sign is in effect only when the lights are on.

WORK SITE LIGHTS

Work site lights warn road users of areas where road mainte-nance or repairs are being carried out. Road users must slow down and be cautious when nearing the work area.

SIGNAL BEACON

A flashing or rotating yellow light on a vehicle indicates one of the following to road users:

- the vehicle could hinder traffic;
- the vehicle might travel much slower than the maximum speed limit or slower than the minimum speed limit;
- the vehicle could be accompanying another vehicle which might hinder traffic.

SIGNAL LIGHTS

SIGNAL ARROWS

An arrow affixed to a vehicle or trailer indicates to road users that one lane of traffic is obstructed and that they must take the lane which remains open. The direction of the arrow indicates the lane to use. A double arrow indicates that traffic can go to the left or right of the obstructed lane. To indicate the presence of a work site along a road with one lane of traffic in each direction, only the centre bar of the signal arrow is lit.

MOUNTED SIGNS WITH FLASHING LIGHTS FOR MOBILE ROAD WORK

Mounted signs with flashing lights are placed on the back of vehicles trailing mobile road works. They are made up of a work site sign mounted on a black background with flashing yellow lights in each corner.

TEMPORARY LIGHTS FOR ROAD WORK

Temporary lights are sometimes placed near a work area to control traffic, which must use one lane alternately for travel in opposite directions.

SIGNAL LIGHTS

BUS PRIORITY LIGHTS

This additional traffic light has a white vertical bar shining through a black lens, indicating protected movement for buses so they can more easily merge with the flow of traffic.

INSPECTION STATION LIGHTS

These lights are placed in an inspection area for transport vehicles. The colour and symbol on the signal light indicate to heavy vehicle drivers what action is necessary.

- Red light:
  stop for weighing.
- Yellow light pointing up:
  advance slowly.
- Yellow light pointing right:
  enter the weighing station.
- Yellow arrow pointing down:
  back up slowly.
- Green light:
  weighing complete, departure permitted.

PAVEMENT MARKINGS

Pavement markings are used to show the separation of traffic lanes, indicate the lanes to be used by certain classes of vehicles and the movements that are authorized. They supplement road signs and traffic signals.

PURPOSE OF PAVEMENT MARKINGS

Pavement markings indicate:

- the direction of traffic;
- traffic lanes;
- zones where passing is prohibited;
- the edge of the roadway and dangerous curbs;
- variations in roadway width;
- zones reserved for buses and heavy vehicles;
- edges of intersections;
- stop lines;
- pedestrian, school and playground crosswalks;
- parking areas;
- commercial service areas;
- special manoeuvres as indicated by arrows;
- obstructions on or next to the road ahead;
- alternating traffic lanes;
- cycle lanes;
- reserved lanes;
- left-turn lanes;
- runaway lanes.

COLOUR OF PAVEMENT MARKINGS

Two colours are used to differentiate the function of each. They are yellow and white.

Yellow markings

- separate traffic lanes in opposite directions;
- indicate the left side of the road on divided roadways, freeways (autoroutes) and one-way roadways;
- indicate the left edge of a ramp on freeways;
- indicate areas where parking is prohibited;
- indicate areas where children, pedestrians and students must cross between intersections or intersections for which there is no traffic light or stop sign;
- indicate the edges of the roadway for better visibility;
- separate alternate traffic lanes;
- indicate two-way left-turn lanes;
- indicate lanes reserved for oncoming or alternate traffic.

White markings

- separate traffic lanes on a one-way roadway;
- indicate the right side of divided roadways;
- indicate parking areas;
- indicate areas where pedestrians, children and students must cross at intersections for which there is no traffic light or stop sign;
- specify where vehicles must stop;
- indicate lanes reserved for traffic in the same direction.

PAVEMENT MARKINGS

LINES, ARROWS AND SYMBOLS

White or yellow lines, as well as arrows and other symbols, are painted on Québec roadways to remind vehicle operators of certain rights, obligations and restrictions. Each type and colour of line has a particular significance.

SOLID AND BROKEN SINGLE LINES

Solid and broken single lines divide traffic lanes. The lines are white when separating one-way traffic lanes and yellow when separating two-way traffic lanes.

Motorists may cross a broken line under certain circumstances but may never cross a solid line.

COMBINED LINES

Two solid yellow lines next to one another separate two-way traffic lanes. They may not be crossed. A solid yellow line alongside a broken yellow line also separates two-way traffic. Drivers may cross these lines under certain circumstances, if the broken line is on their side.

LANE LINES

Lines that separate lanes of traffic in the same direction are generally white and broken; however, in order to limit or prohibit lane changes, the lines may be solid, single or double, such as at the approach of another roadway or in a tunnel.

ALTERNATING TRAFFIC LANE USES

Parallel yellow broken lines mark a lane on either side in urban areas where the direction of traffic alternates.

TWO-WAY LEFT-TURN LANE

Parallel yellow lines, one solid and one broken, mark a lane on either side in the middle of the roadway which must be used for left turns by traffic in opposite directions. Yellow lane selection arrows also mark the pavement to clearly indicate that only a left turn is allowed from the lane.

RESERVED LANE

Pavement markings for a reserved lane at all times are double solid lines, while those marking a reserved lane for certain hours are double broken lines. Wedges on the pavement in the reserved lane tell motorists in the adjacent lane that shared use of the lane is allowed on condition they turn at the nearby intersection.

SLOW-MOVING VEHICLE LANE

A lane is set aside at places where the grade of a slope or its length causes some heavy vehicles to slow considerably, allowing the freer movement of the bulk of traffic.

STOP LINE

The white stop line is painted across the roadway, perpendicular to an intersection with traffic lights or a stop sign. It indicates the point at which a vehicle must stop.

PAVEMENT MARKINGS

PAVEMENT MARKINGS

PEDESTRIAN CROSSWALKS

At intersections with traffic lights or stop signs, two parallel solid white lines on the roadway indicate the area reserved for pedestrians to cross. Elsewhere, yellow pavement markings indicate pedestrian crosswalks.

PARKING AREAS

White lines on the pavement identify areas where parking is allowed; yellow lines indicate that parking is prohibited.

WHEELCHAIR

A white wheelchair symbol indicates parking spaces or access ramps for persons with physical disabilities. It is accompanied by a regulatory parking sign on parking spaces, indicating that these parking spaces are reserved exclusively for physically disabled individuals.

BUS STOP ZONE

Stop zones for city buses are marked by a yellow rectangle with a zigzag pattern. The left side of the rectangle is marked with a white broken line.

VEHICLE SENSOR

This symbol on the pavement indicates a mechanism connected to traffic lights to sense the presence of vehicles. The symbol is placed on the centre of the sensor and is designed to reduce waiting time at intersections.

Aircraft Patrolled

Yellow equilateral triangles on the pavement or shoulder denote areas where traffic is subject to surveillance from aircraft.

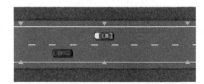

Arrows and Symbols

Arrows, usually white are painted on the roadway. They indicate lane direction.

An elongated white diamond on pavement indicates a lane reserved for certain classes of vehicles.

A bicycle symbol painted on the roadway indicates a cycling lane.

ROAD SIGNS

ROAD SIGNS

Road signs use a visual language (pictograms and inscriptions) to ensure road users' safety and facilitate the flow of traffic.

In many instances, the tab attached to a sign specifies the message conveyed by the road sign.

There are four types of road signs:

Regulatory signs

Regulatory signs indicate road users' obligations and the restrictions placed upon them under the *Highway Safety Code*.

Warning signs

Warning signs are meant to draw attention to road sections where drivers must be particularly cautious due to obstacles or hazards on or alongside the roadway. The signs warn motorists to slow down, stop or change directions.

Information signs

Information signs provide simple directions about destinations: distance, street name, point of interest, service or information.

Road work signs

Work site signs draw attention to construction or maintenance being carried out on or alongside a roadway and provide useful indications on how to get through the work area safely. These signs encompass the purpose of the three prior categories.

SHAPES AND COLOURS OF THE MAIN TYPES OF SIGNS

The message conveyed by a road sign depends on the shape, colour or symbol used.

The choice of colour takes North American conventions into account. In general, the colours that follow allow one to distinguish between the different categories of signs:

Black and white: Regulatory signs

Yellow: Danger

Orange: Road work sign

Green, brown or blue: Information sign

Sometimes the shape of a sign identifies its category. For example, danger and work site signs are diamond shaped. In addition, some shapes are reserved for particular signs. For example, an octagon is reserved for stop signs and a pentagon is reserved solely to identify school zones.

Regulatory, warning and road work signs transmit their messages using arrows and symbols, whereas information signs bear written information.

This table specifies the shapes and colours of the four sign categories.

Category	Shape	Colour	Comments
Regulatory		Red	Reserved for *stop signs*
		Red and white	Reserved for *yield signs*
		Black	
		White	
		Black	Reserved for *one-way signs*

ROAD SIGNS

Category	Shapes	Colour	Comments
Warning and road work		Fluorescent yellow-green	Reserved for *school zone signs*
		Fluorescent yellow-green	Reserved for *advance school zone* or *school crossing signs*
		Yellow	Reserved for *danger warning*
		Orange	Reserved for *work sites*
		Yellow	Danger warning
		Orange	Work sites
		Yellow	Danger warning
		Orange	Work sites
		Red and white	Reserved for *warning chevrons*

Category	Shapes	Colour	Comments
Information		Blue	Reserved for *freeways*
		Green	Reserved for *highways*
		Blue	Tourist information
		Brown	Public tourist attractions
		Red	Emergency facilities
		Green	Freeways, highways and bikeways
		Green	Freeways, highways and bikeways
		Blue	Private facilities and services off freeways
		Brown	Tourist attractions and points of interest
		Yellow	Reserved for *freeway exits*

PICTOGRAPHS

Symbols such as pictographs, arrows and silhouettes are used to replace words in order to make road signs easier to understand.

• Arrows

Arrows are used to indicate areas controlled by regulation, to announce upcoming signs, and to indicate clearances, lanes to follow or use, detours, manoeuvres and destinations.

• Outlines

Silhouettes indicate the people and things affected by the sign. They indicate specific configurations, encourage road users to be particularly careful, and convey information.

• Interdictory symbol

This symbol, a red circle with a red diagonal bar through it, indicates that anything within the circle is prohibited.

• Mandatory symbol

This symbol, a green circle, indicates that anything within the circle is compulsory.

REGULATORY SIGNS

IDENTIFICATION AND MEANING
OF ROAD SIGNS AND TRAFFIC SIGNALS

Regulatory signs

Stop

Indicates that drivers must come to a full stop at an intersection.

4-way stop: indicates that the requirement to stop applies to traffic from all directions. The shape on the sign identifies the layout of the intersection (**+, T, Y**).

Do not enter

Indicates that access to a roadway or traffic lane is prohibited for all vehicles because entry could result in a head-on collision.

Accompanied by an "ENTREE INTERDITE" (do not enter) sign.

Yield

Indicates that drivers must yield the right of way to vehicles travelling on the road they are about to enter.

REGULATORY SIGNS

Traffic circle yield: Indicates that drivers must yield the right of way to vehicles that are travelling in the traffic circle they are about to enter. When encountering these signs, some drivers believe they can continue driving normally. By way of contrast, other drivers systematically come to a full stop. Both unwittingly disrupt the flow or traffic. The objective here is to merge with traffic without stopping, and without hampering the progress of those who are already in place. Motorists should only stop when it is impossible to do otherwise.

Indicates that drivers must yield the right of way to oncoming vehicles. This sign is used at work sites where no flagperson is available, and on some narrow bridges.

Stop line

Indicates the line on the roadway at which vehicles must stop.

REGULATORY SIGNS

Speed limit

Indicates the maximum and minimum speeds legally permitted.

The last digit is always zero.

Indicates the speed that applies, under the *Highway Safety Code* or municipal bylaw, to a school zone and the hours, day and months during which the speed limit is in effect.

One-way traffic

Traffic is allowed only in the direction indicated.

Beginning of one-way traffic

Indicates that two-way traffic ends and one-way traffic begins.

Two-way traffic

Indicates that one-way traffic ends and two-way traffic begins.

Obstruction

Indicates that a driver must go to the right to pass an obstacle.

Indicates that a driver must go to the left to pass an obstacle.

Indicates an obstacle which must be passed either to the right or left.

Lane direction signs

Whether placed overhead or along the roadway, the following signs indicate the direction of travel allowed, depending on the lane occupied by the motorist.

REGULATORY SIGNS

These signs indicate that the vehicle in the lane must:

Proceed
straight ahead

Turn right

Turn left

Proceed straight ahead or turn right.
Proceed straight ahead or turn left.

Turn right or left.

VOIE DU CENTRE

The centre lane is reserved for left turns from either direction.

Vehicles in right lane must proceed straight ahead; vehicles in left lane must turn left.

Vehicles in right lane must turn right; vehicles in left lane must proceed straight ahead.

Vehicles in the right lane must proceed straight ahead; vehicles in left lane must proceed straight ahead or turn left.

Vehicles in the right lane may proceed straight ahead or turn right; vehicles in the left lane must proceed straight ahead.

Vehicles in the right lane may proceed straight ahead or turn right; vehicles in left lane must turn left.

Vehicles in the right lane must turn right; vehicles in the left lane may proceed straight ahead or turn left.

Vehicles in the right lane may proceed straight ahead or turn left; vehicles in the left lane must turn left.

Vehicles in the right lane must turn right; vehicles in the left lane may proceed straight ahead or turn right.

Vehicles in the right and centre lanes must proceed straight ahead; vehicles in the left lane must turn left.

REGULATORY SIGNS

Vehicles in the right lane must turn right; vehicles in the left and centre lanes must proceed straight ahead.

Vehicles in the two right-hand lanes must turn right.

Vehicles in the two left-hand lanes must turn left.

Vehicles in the left lane must turn left; vehicles in the right lane may turn right, proceed straight ahead or turn left.

Vehicles in the left lane may turn right, proceed straight ahead or turn left; vehicles in the right lane must turn right.

NB Some signs with black arrows on a white background will continue to be used until replaced with signs that have a black background by June 30, 2006 in accordance with new standards.

Alternating traffic lane

An alternating traffic lane is one where the direction allowed will vary with traffic conditions or the time of day. In the illustration, it is the centre lane.

The signs installed above the roadway show available lanes.

A driver may use the lane underneath a green arrow.

A red X over a lane indicates that it is reserved for oncoming traffic.

Mandatory or prohibited movement at certain intersections

The green circles mean that vehicle operators must comply with the manoeuvre shown on the circle.

A. These signs indicate that the operator **must**:

Proceed
straight ahead

Turn left

Turn right

REGULATORY SIGNS

Proceed
straight ahead
or turn right

Proceed
straight ahead
or turn left

Turn right
or left

B. These signs indicate that the driver **may not**:

Proceed
straight ahead

Turn left

Turn right

Make a U-turn at an intersection or median.

Turn right when the light is red. If the prohibition is limited to specific time periods, they will be indicated.

Indicate that the prohibited or required manoeuvre is temporary or does not apply to certain classes of vehicles. The exception to the U-turn prohibition means that emergency vehicles, public security vehicles and road construction or maintenance vehicles are allowed to use the turn-around area.

No passing

Indicates the beginning of a no-passing zone.

This tab, located beneath a no-passing sign, indicates the end of a no-passing zone.

Controlled parking

Indicate areas where parking is prohibited or permitted. Where specified, different symbols or indications identify the classes of vehicles, minutes, hours, days, months or extent of the zone to which the sign applies (identified by an arrow).

REGULATORY SIGNS

Indicates areas where parking is allowed only for the physically disabled.

This tab, located beneath regulated parking signs, indicates that vehicles in violation could be towed away.

This signs, used in some municipalities, prohibits parking during the winter.

This sign is used in conjunction with orange lights to prohibit parking when snow clearing is under way.

This sign indicates authorized pay parking.

This tab indicates the location of a terminal and parking stub machine for pay parking.

No stopping

Stopping in the area indicated by the sign is prohibited. May include the same type of arrows and indications as regulated parking signs.

Crossing signs

Indicate a crossing for people on a public roadway, urging caution on the part of motorists and cyclists. Drivers and bicycle riders must be prepared to stop and yield the way to anyone in a crosswalk.

Pedestrian
crosswalk

School
crosswalk

Playground
crosswalk

Crosswalk
for physically
disabled persons

Crosswalk
for visually
impaired persons

Pedestrian
and cyclist
crosswalk

REGULATORY SIGNS

REGULATORY SIGNS

Other

 No littering. Indicates that throwing anything on the roadway is prohibited.

 Shows the fine for littering.

 Indicates that vehicles are prohibited from having radar warning devices on board.

 FERMEZ ET SCELLEZ — Indicate the obligation of having propane tanks closed and sealed in order to board a ferry.

Seat belt

A reminder that wearing a properly fastened seat belt is mandatory.

Mandatory route for certain classes of vehicles

Shows operators of the class of vehicle illustrated the route they must follow.

Heavy trucks   Motorcycles   Cars

 An arrow shows the direction of compulsory travel.

Mandatory route for trucks in transit

An arrow shows the direction of compulsory travel for trucks in transit; a truck is considered to be in transit over an area where no local deliveries are scheduled. Tool vehicles and equipment transport vehicles are also covered by the obligation. Farm vehicles and machinery are allowed to use the route, as is any oversized vehicle with a special travel permit.

NB The same type of sign is used to indicate other directions.

REGULATORY SIGNS

Allows trucks to use a roadway to make local deliveries that is normally prohibited to vehicles in transit.

This sign over a lane tells drivers of heavy trucks, tool vehicles and equipment transport vehicles that they must use the lane. Where this lane continues for more than 2 km, a tab indicates the total distance.

Access prohibited

Indicate that roads or lanes are closed to certain road users or operators of certain classes of vehicles.

Cars

Motorcycles

Bicycles

Cars and
motorcycles

Cars and
bicycles

All-terrain vehicles
(also called
Quads)

Pedestrians

Pedestrians and
motorcycles

Pedestrians
and bicycles

Horseback
riders

Snowmobiles

Transit bus

Intercity bus

Minibus

School bus

In-line skaters

Recreational
vehicles

Vehicles
pulling a trailer

REGULATORY SIGNS

Trucks, tool vehicles and equipment transport vehicles prohibited

These signs indicate that use of the roadway is restricted according to the vehicle's load, size or number of axles and pertains to trucks, tool vehicles and equipment transport vehicles. Where specified, this prohibition does not apply to trucks making a local delivery.

This sign allows trucks to use a normally prohibited roadway and side streets to make local deliveries.

No trucks allowed in this lane.

....

Transport of hazardous material

These signs indicate that vehicles hauling hazardous materials must use the route indicated or that they are prohibited from using a roadway. Mainly intended for industrial and commercial carriers, who should be aware of their obligations. The signs may concern individual motorists if they are carrying an unusual amount of fuel, explosives and chemicals.

Vehicles carrying hazardous materials must use this route, which is identified by a tab with an arrow.

Vehicles carrying hazardous materials are prohibited from using this roadway.

This sign indicates that vehicles carrying hazardous materials must use this lane.

Vehicles carrying hazardous materials must not use this lane.

Stop exemption at a level crossing

Indicate that vehicles normally required to stop at a level crossing, such as buses and vehicles carrying hazardous materials, are not required to do so. The signs are used near abandoned tracks or ones on which rail traffic is infrequent and special measures have been put into place to ensure safety when there is train movement.

REGULATORY SIGNS

Weight restriction

  Indicates that road vehicles whose gross weight exceeds the maximum weight indicated on the sign may not use certain bridges or overpasses.

 This tab, located under the weight restriction sign, indicates the distance to the bridge or overpass to which the restriction applies.

 This tab, located under the weight restriction sign, indicates that the bridge or overpass can only support one such vehicle at a time.

 Indicates that trucks whose gross weight exceeds the legal limit may not use certain bridges or overpasses unless expressly authorized by a special travel permit.

Thaw

 Indicates that drivers must respect the weight restrictions in effect during periods of thaw.

REGULATORY SIGNS

Slow traffic lane

Indicates that operators of slow-moving vehicles, whether trucks or other vehicles, must use the right-hand lane.

Brake check

Indicates that drivers of road vehicles or combination vehicles weighing 3,000 kg or more must check their brakes by stopping in the area indicated by a stop sign.

A tab may indicate the distance or direction to the brake check area.

This sign, installed in a brake check area, indicates that there is a stop sign within 30 metres.

Inspection station

Indicates the presence of an inspection station for heavy trucks, tow trucks, equipment transport vehicles, tool vehicles and vehicles with a trailer or semi-trailer more than 10 m in length.

These tabs indicate the distance and direction to the weighing check point at an inspection station.

Indicates that the driver of a straight-body truck or road tractor whose net weight is over 3,000 kg must stop at the inspection station when the lights are flashing.

Indicates the direction to be taken by vehicles at an inspection station according to whether they are loaded or not.

Reserved lanes

An elongated white diamond on a red or black background in the upper left-hand corner of the sign indicates a reserved lane.

Black background

Indicates that vehicles in the reserved lane move in the direction of traffic.

Red background

Indicates that the lane is reserved for oncoming traffic or for alternating traffic in either direction.

Indicates that a lane is reserved for the classes of users indicated and, if applicable, the period the reserved lane is in effect. The arrow indicates which lane is reserved.

Marks the end of reserved lanes.

The car-pool symbol shows a number on the silhouette of a vehicle, indicating the minimum number of occupants a vehicle must have for it to be allowed use of the reserved lane.

Warning signs

Warning signs do not all demand the same response from drivers. Depending on the circumstances, vehicle operators must:

- change lane;
- stop;
- reduce speed;
- remain alert and vigilant.

Advance stop sign

Warns of a stop sign ahead.

Advance yield sign

Warns of a yield sign ahead.

WARNING SIGNS

Warns of a yield to oncoming traffic sign ahead.

Change to existing signs and new signs

This type of sign warns drivers of a change to existing signs or of new traffic control devices at an intersection.

 Indicates the date on which a stop sign will be removed.

 Indicates the date on which a stop sign will come into effect.

Show the position of new stop signs at an intersection. These are accompanied by tab a reading "NOUVELLE SIGNALISATION" (new sign).

NB The word STOP may replace ARRÊT in the above signs.

WARNING SIGNS

 Indicates the date on which traffic lights will be removed.

Indicates the date on which traffic lights will be in service.

 Indicates the date on which a new lower speed limit will come into effect.

 Indicates new traffic lights or sign.

Indicates change of speed limit, placed under the sign showing the limit.

Advance warning of traffic lights

 Traffic lights ahead.

Prepare to stop

Traffic lights ahead at an intersection or level crossing on a roadway where one might not expect to see them. The flashing yellow lights indicate that the light at the intersection or level crossing will be red by the time the driver reaches it. It is important to be prepared to stop.

Advance speed limit sign

Indicates a zone ahead where the speed limit has been lowered by at least 30 km/h.

When an *advance sign* is used before the approach of a school zone where a speed limit is in effect during specific periods, this tab specifies the time, days and months the speed limit is in effect.

Two-way traffic

Indicates two-way traffic ahead.

WARNING SIGNS

Divided roadway

 Warns the driver of a divided roadway ahead and to pass to the right.

 Indicates that the driver may pass on either side of an obstacle in the roadway.

 Indicates the end of a divided roadway.

Advance lane direction signs

These signs indicate which lane the driver must take in order to proceed straight ahead or turn.

VOIE DE DROITE

VOIE DU CENTRE

NB The same type of sign is used for left-handed turns.

Curves

 Warns of left curve ahead.

 Warns of sharp left curve ahead.

 Warns of reverse curve ahead.

 Warns of sharp reverse curve ahead.

 Winding road ahead; three or more successive curves within 150 m of one another.

 Indicates the distance over which there are curves, if it exceeds 1 km.

 Warns of curve of more than 90° ahead.

WARNING SIGNS

Recommended speed

Tab showing recommended speed when driving around an obstacle or taking a curve on a public road.

NB The same type of sign is used for right-handed turns or successive curves that begin on the right.

Maximum recommended speed on freeway exit ramps, which allows for enough of a safety margin to make an emergency stop on wet pavement.

Merging traffic sign

Warns of merging traffic lanes ahead.

Warns of a traffic lane reserved for buses merging ahead.

Parallel lanes

Indicates to drivers that there are one or more distinct adjacent traffic lanes, so there is no need to change lanes for at least 1 km.

NB Merging lanes or parallel lanes may be on the left or right.

Signs at intersections

The sign indicates the layout of the intersection.

Crossroad ahead.

T-intersection ahead.

The following signs indicate the approach of the location where the public road intersects with another as seen from the angle of the driver.

Y-intersection ahead.

T-intersection in a curve ahead.

Intersection of a road divided by a median ahead.

Roundabout ahead, showing direction of vehicles around a traffic circle.

WARNING SIGNS

Narrow passage

Warns that a bridge or tunnel is narrower than the approach.

Warns that only one lane is open to traffic and that the roadway is no more than 6 metres wide.

Overhead clearance sign

Indicate the overhead clearance of bridges, overpasses and tunnels. The diamond-shape sign is an advance warning. The square sign is placed on the bridge, overpass or tunnel.

Advance level crossing sign

Level crossings less than 50 metres from an intersection in urban areas and less than 125 metres in rural areas.

The signs below warn of a level crossing ahead and show the angle at which the railway tracks cross the road.

 This sign is installed to warn truckers of a level crossing ahead and requires them to significantly reduce their speed because of the crossing design.

Restricted visibility

  Indicate that sight distance is limited or non-existent due to an abrupt slope in the road.

Roadway narrows

Indicate that the roadway narrows without a reduction in the number of lanes. Calls for added attention on the part of drivers. Not to be confused with lane ending signs.

| Warns that roadway narrows on both sides | Warns that roadway narrows on the right | Warns that roadway narrows on the left |

Lane ends ahead

Indicate that the number of lanes of traffic in the same direction is reduced. Calls on drivers in the lane about to end to change lanes after yielding the right of way to vehicles in the through lane. Not to be confused with roadway narrows signs.

NB Signs may indicate that the lane ends on the left rather than the right.

This tab indicates the distance at which the lane ends.

Pavement markings may accompany these signs.

Lane or road ends

Warns of the end of a roadway or lane.

Steep grade

Indicates the slope in percentage terms (at least 6%, which means a drop of 6 m over 100 m). The higher the percentage, the steeper the hill; requires greater caution from all drivers, especially of heavy vehicles, in the event of a slippery road surface or winding hills.

Indicates the maximum degree of slope in percentage.

Indicates a slope ahead with a length of more than one kilometre.

These signs are used for two successive hills with different degrees of slope. The total distance is indicated if it exceeds 1 km.

Reserved lane ahead

Indicate that the lane ahead is reserved for the use of a particular class of vehicle. The flashing lights indicate that the restriction is in effect and the tab indicates the period during which it is in effect.

Indicates that the lane at an intersection is reserved for the use of a particular class of vehicle, and right-turning vehicles must use the adjacent lane.

School bus ahead

Indicates the possible presence of a stopped school bus ahead. This sign is used where a curve or hill impedes a driver's line of sight of a stopped school bus, indicating that they must be prepared to stop. Warns of the possible presence of children near the roadway.

Beginning of a school zone

Indicates the presence of a school zone in which the speed limit is 50 km/h between 7:00 a.m. and 5:00 p.m., Monday to Friday, from September to June. If some municipalities prescribe a limit of less than 50 km/h in a school zone, a speed limit sign will accompany this sign indicating the speed limit, times, days and months the limit is in effect. A sign posting the speed limit outside of the school zone indicates the end of the school zone.

WARNING SIGNS

Advance crossing signs

These signs warn motorists that they are nearing a crossing for pedestrians, bicycles, horses or certain types of vehicles.

Pedestrian
crosswalk ahead

School
crosswalk ahead

Playground
crosswalk ahead

Crosswalk
for disabled
persons ahead

Crossing for
visually impaired
persons ahead

Bicycle
crossing ahead

Pedestrian
and cyclist
crosswalk ahead

Heavy truck
crossing ahead

Logging
trucks ahead

Snowmobile
crossing ahead

All-terrain
vehicle crossing
ahead

Crossing
for horseback
riders ahead

All-terrain vehicle and snowmobile crossings ahead

   Warning of wild animals in the vicinity.

  Crossing for farm animals

Designated shared roadway

 Indicates to cyclists and drivers that they must share the designated roadway, which calls for caution and courtesy on the part of each.

Advance designated roadway sign

Warns of a change from a cycle lane to a roadway that includes motor vehicles, or indicates a designated roadway ahead.

Advance end of freeway (autoroute) sign

These signs indicate the distance remaining before the freeway ends and indicates the layout of the road at the location the freeway ends.

Hazard markers

Warn of the presence of obstacles on or along the roadway ahead, as well as the narrowing of a road. Diagonal bands point towards the side of the roadway the driver must use to avoid the hazard, which may be an obstacle such as a boulder or bridge railing.

Indicates that the driver must pass to the right or left of obstacles.

Indicates that the driver must go to the right to pass the obstacle.

WARNING SIGNS

Indicates that the driver must go to the left to pass the obstacle.

Directional arrows

Indicates a dangerous point in a very sharp curve or at a T-intersection. Sharper curves are marked with delineators or chevron patterns.

Delineator

Placed on left   Placed on right

Marks the boundaries of any obstacle or the edge of a roadway, especially on curves or where it narrows. Effective in guiding road users at night or in poor visibility, especially when the pavement is wet or snow-covered. An arrow points in the direction of a curve; sharp curves are indicated with alignment markers.

WARNING SIGNS

Alignment marker

The chevron pattern is used to indicate a sharp curve, pointing in the direction of the curve.

Installed at the centre of a traffic circle, this sign indicates the direction of traffic within the circle.

Slippery surface

Warns that the road surface in certain areas may be slippery when wet.

Warns that a roadway along the shore may be slippery due to sea spray.

Warns motorcycle operators that the road surface may be slippery when wet.

Icy pavement

Warns that a roadway, bridge or overpass may become icy or slippery when the temperature approaches freezing.

Flooded roadway

Warns that water covers the roadway at certain points.

Pavement change

Warns of grooved pavement ahead or wire-mesh surface on a bridge.

End of paved surface

Warns that pavement ends and a gravel or dirt surface begins.

Bumpy road ahead

Warns of surface irregularities.

Fallen rock hazard

Warns of the possibility of falling rock or landslides from an unstable slope alongside a roadway.

Opening bridge ahead

Indicates the presence of a drawbridge.

Low-flying aircraft

These signs indicate the possibility of low-flying aircraft manoeuvres near the roadway.

Major airport

Certified public or private airport

Seaplane base

Heliport

WARNING SIGNS

No entry ahead for trucks except local delivery

Indicates that access to the roadway ahead is prohibited for trucks except those making local deliveries.

Risk of getting stuck

Indicates that a vehicle could get stuck if it went further ahead; usually found at runaway lane stop beds.

Fog warning

Warns of a possibility of fog; the flashing lights indicate the presence of fog.

Blowing snow

Warns against the possible presence of snow on a public roadway; the flashing lights indicate snow blown by high winds.

Be visible

Warns that vehicle headlights and tail-lights must be on when using a tunnel.

Road work signs

Work site signs have an orange background. They may be regulatory, information or warning in nature.

Barriers

 When work is in progress, barriers close part or all of a road to traffic. They are placed at the beginning of a work site.

Visual markers

Visual markers indicate the boundaries of a work site (area where work is in progress) or narrowing of a roadway before a work site. They show the direction to follow, indicate road painting in progress or direct traffic.

Direction marker

Painting marker

Work site marker

Traffic cone

Safety flare

Barrel

Distance to road construction site

Indicates the distance to a work site.

Distance to end of work site

Indicates length of work site in kilometres.

Indicates end of work site.

Speed limit

Sign indicating the maximum speed permitted near a work site; unlike the yellow background, which would indicate a recommended speed, the orange sign with black lettering shows the speed limit authorized in the area, and has the same force of law as the usual white sign with black lettering.

The diamond-shaped sign indicates the new speed limit ahead.

ROAD WORK SIGNS

Road work signs

Indicate the presence of a work site ahead and the type of work being carried out.

People working

Surveying

Heavy
equipment
in use

Equipment
working above
roadway

Indicates the distance the work site covers in kilometres.

Indicate that a grader or snowblower is operating in a traffic lane or nearby.

Indicates that an emergency response team is on or alongside the road.

This sign, placed on an accompanying vehicle, warns of stalled traffic due to road work.

Indicates that a road is closed due to a sporting event.

Flagperson's sign

FRONT   BACK

Used to slow or stop traffic. The front and back of a person's sign is used to control traffic near a work site.

A flag may be used for the same purpose.

Flagperson's signals

Stop

Proceed

Slow down

ROAD WORK SIGNS

Flagperson ahead

Warns of the presence of a flagperson ahead directing traffic. Calls for caution because traffic is slowed, detoured or stopped temporarily due to road work. A flagperson's orders must be obeyed.

Parking temporarily prohibited

These signs prohibit parking for a time on the road to facilitate road work, special events or maintenance operations.

The sign may indicate the times, days and area when parking is prohibited.

Area ahead temporarily closed to traffic

Indicate that an area ahead such as a road, street, tunnel, exit or bridge is temporally closed to traffic.

Area temporarily closed to traffic

Indicate that an area is temporarily closed to traffic. Accompanied by detour signs.

Local traffic only

Indicates that the roadway is closed to all but nearby residents and business customers. It may also indicate which services remain available.

Lane merge

This type of sign indicates that one lane is temporarily closed and that the one remaining open must be used.

ROAD WORK SIGNS

Detour

Indicate the route to follow around a road work site.

Indicate the route to take due to closure of a traffic lane or exit.

Alternate route

Indicate the alternate route suggested to highway users in view of the risks of congestion associated with work ahead.

Arrow

Indicates the direction traffic must take.

Warning chevron

Indicates that an obstacle on the roadway may be passed to the left or right.

Low shoulder

Indicates that the shoulder is lower than the roadway.

Blasting zone

For safety reasons, radio transmitters and cell phones should be turned off in a blasting zone.

ROAD WORK SIGNS

Wet paint

Installed primarily on an accompanying vehicle, this sign warns that pavement markings have been freshly painted.

Installed on the marker vehicle.

Traffic survey

Warn of the presence of survey personnel on the road.

Horizontal clearance

Warns that construction work obstructs part of the roadway and horizontal clearance is less than the road width indicated.

Loose gravel

Warns of the possibility of small debris dislodged by vehicles during or after road work.

Truck crossing ahead

Indicates that a loaded truck may use the roadway from an access road ahead.

Temporary use of road shoulder

Indicate that traffic is allowed or prohibited temporarily on the road shoulder near a work site.

Duration of road work

Indicates the period during which road work will be ongoing.

Lane diverted

Traffic must detour because of work ahead.

NB The same type of sign is used for a detour to the right.

Information signs

There are six types of these signs:

- **destination guide;**
- **route locator;**
- **off-road services;**
- **information;**
- **tourist facilities;**
- **fuel and food services on freeways.**

Destinations

Advance sign for several exits for a municipality

Indicates that the freeway passes through a municipality served by a succession of interchanges. The sign shows the number of exits and the distance to the last exit.

Succession of exits

Indicates upcoming exits and their distance away.

Advance exit sign

Indicates the number of the connecting road ahead, the main destinations from the interchange, the exit number and distance to the exit.

Directional sign for exits

Confirms the information appearing on advance exit signs and indicates, by means of arrows, the beginning of the interchange exit lane.

Diagrammatic sign

Quickly informs the driver of the direction to take at an interchange with more than one exit.

Confirmation of destination

Indicates the destination of a freeway and lane use to take that route.

Exit lane only sign

Advance
exit sign

Exit
direction

Exit
confirmation

Indicate that a traffic lane leads directly to a freeway exit ramp. Exit lanes are identified by a series of three signs so that drivers have time to change lanes before they must take the next exit.

Exit sign

Indicate the beginning of the exit ramp, its direction and the exit number.

Directional sign

Indicate the major destination that can be reached by taking a particular direction at an intersection.

Distance reminder

Confirm the direction and shows the distance to reach the destination indicated.

Lakeshore community

Indicates the presence of a lake with cottages, the direction to take and the distance.

Route locator

Highways

Marker

Expressway,
freeway
(autoroute)

Trans-Canada
Highway

Expressway,
freeway name

Highway name

Roads and tourist routes

Indicates a road or tourist route and directs
road users.

Indicates the start of a road or tourist route.

INFORMATION SIGNS

INFORMATION SIGNS

Border

The two following signs indicate to drivers that they are entering the provincial boundaries of Québec.

Marks the Québec boundary on routes 100 to 199, on freeways and at the exit of international airports.

Marks the Québec boundary on routes 200 to 399 or on unnumbered roads.

Shows the name of the tourism area in which the road user is entering.

Indicates the limits of a community or Indian reserve.

Bridge

Indicates the location of a bridge and its name as it appears on official Québec road maps.

Compass points

These signs indicate the general direction of the road.

They may appear with a blue background.

End of freeway or highway

End of freeway, which continues as another numbered highway.

Indicating the end of a numbered highway or freeway, which continues under another number and is accompanied with an information sign of the numbered highway or freeway.

Distance

Tab showing the distance to reach a specific facility or road feature.

Directional arrow tabs

Tabs indicating the direction of an freeway, numbered highway or to a particular facility.

Tabs indicating the general direction of numbered highway. The arrow points in the direction to follow.

INFORMATION SIGNS

Junction

Tab indicating the intersection of a numbered highway.

Kilometre post

Marks the distance from the starting point of a highway or road.

Marks the beginning and end of an isolated road

Geographic locations

The name of lakes, rivers, mountains, waterfalls and water storage dams visible from the road.

Mont ROUGEMONT   Réservoir CABONGA   Rivière RICHELIEU

Lac MÉGANTIC   Chute LYSANDER

Services

Emergency facilities

Police station

Indicates a Sûreté du Québec (provincial police force) station.

Indicates a police station other than a Sûreté du Québec station.

Shows the telephone numbers to reach the Sûreté du Québec.

Medical assistance

Indicates a nearby hospital, university health centre or emergency station providing 24-hour medical care.

Indicates a nearby community clinic.

Emergency parking area

Indicates a freeway parking area for use in the event of an emergency.

INFORMATION SIGNS

INFORMATION SIGNS

Emergency telephone

Indicates the presence of an emergency telephone.

Fire hydrant

Indicates a fire hydrant and its features.

Vehicle in distress

Indicates that a vehicle needs assistance, having broken through a barrier and plunged into a deep ditch along an isolated stretch of road. A mechanism triggers the sign, which calls for the help of road users, who should act immediately to help and notify the police.

Transport facilities

This sign directs road users to the facilities illustrated.

INFORMATION SIGNS

Airport

Indicates the presence of an airport with a fixed flight schedule, the front of the plane pointing in the direction to follow.

Indicates the presence of an airport offering certain services.

Seaplane base.

Heliport

Indicates the direction of an airport (or train station) and its name.

Indicates the name of an airport (or train station), direction to follow and distance.

Train station

Indicates a nearby train station.

INFORMATION SIGNS

Indicates a nearby intercity bus station.

Ferry

Indicates the direction or distance to a car ferry wharf and point of departure and arrival.

  Tab indicating ferry operation has ended for the season.

Parking area

Parking area for intermodal transport users.

Suburban train   City bus

Ferry   Subway station

Passenger pickup area

Indicates where drivers can wait for or pick up passengers at a public transit terminal.

Parking area

Parking areas, reserved or accessible to all motor vehicles.

For all motor vehicles

Reserved
for taxis

Reserved
for buses

Reserved for
motorcycles

Reserved
for trucks

Sanitary landfill site

Indicates a sanitary landfill site.

Industrial facilities

Indicates the presence of an industrial park.

INFORMATION SIGNS

Indicates the direction and distance to a technological park.

Indicates the presence of a shipping port.

Boat launch

Indicates the presence of a ramp to launch boats.

Border crossing point

Indicate the presence of a Canada-U.S. border crossing point.

Other facilities

Indicate other services.

Arena

Community centre

Library

Public
market

Church

Indoor public
swimming
pool

Outdoor public
swimming
pool

Municipal
park

College

University

Court house

Information

Dead end

  Indicate a road or street with no exit.

Turnaround

Indicates an area in the median intended for
vehicles to make U-turns.

INFORMATION SIGNS

INFORMATION SIGNS

Priority turn on flashing green

Indicates that vehicle operators facing a flashing green light have the right of way.

Crossing light activator

Indicate to pedestrians and/or cyclists that they must press the crossing light indicator.

An arrow pointing to the left or right may appear on these signs above the button.

Metric signs

Indicates to visitors from the U.S. that Québec road signs use the metric system.

Aircraft patrolled

Indicates the possibility of traffic surveillance from the air.

Runaway lane

Indicates an area where runaway heavy vehicles can be brought to a stop on a steep hill.

Indicates a place where a vehicle with failing brakes may be brought safely to a stop.

Passing lane

Indicates an additional lane to allow for passing.

Distance to service station

Indicates to drivers the distance separating the next fuel services along the road.

Exclusive towing rights

Indicate that towing on a particular section of the highway is handled exclusively by the company whose telephone number appears on the tab.

INFORMATION SIGNS

Public facilities

Rest area

Indicates a rest area run by the Québec government alongside a highway. Services available are shown by the appropriate symbols. A rest area operated by a municipality will be so indicated in place of the fleur-de-lys. The sign may also indicate the distance to the next two rest areas.

Indicates an area for truckers to rest or check their load and vehicle.

Indicates services available, such as a gas station, parking lot, restaurant or any other facility.

Lookout

Indicates a lookout alongside the roadway that offers a splendid view; the field glass points to the lookout.

Covered bridge

Indicates a covered bridge of heritage value.

Reserves, parks and public tourist attractions

Indicate parks under provincial or federal government jurisdiction.

A beaver symbol identifies federal parks or sites.

The maple leaf crown is used to identify parks administered by the National Capital Commission of Canada.

Tourist information

There are four types of tourist information centres: Infotourist offices, local and regional centres and tourist information stands.

Centre operated by Tourism Québec providing information on the province.

Regional tourist information centre providing information about the region.

INFORMATION SIGNS

Local tourist information centre providing information about one or more municipalities. A tab often indicates the direction and distance to the centre.

Indicates a tourist information stand that provides information by means other than staffed personnel.

Foreign currency exchange office.

Private tourist facility

Indicate the presence of a tourist facility, the distance to its access route and the direction to its entrance.

Historic site

Indicates the presence of an historic site, the distance and direction.

Fuel and food service signs on freeways

Confirmation of exits

 Indicates the proximity of a service station and of fuel or food outlets available there.

Itinerary

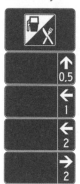 Indicates the direction of facilities alongside a freeway.

Entrance to facility

 Indicate access to facilities.

Types of fuel

  Indicates the types of fuel available other than gasoline, along with the establishment logo or name.

D diesel
N natural gas
P propane

INFORMATION SIGNS

SIGNS FOR CYCLISTS

Off-road cycling route

Indicate a bikeway with an exclusive right-of-way that is separate from automobile traffic and specifies if the route is a recognized *Route verte* (described in section 4.6). The sign indicates if the bikeway is open to another sport in the winter.

SIGNS FOR CYCLISTS

Cyclists are allowed to ride on most roads in Québec other than freeway; motor vehicle operators must therefore exercise caution when they see a bicycle rider on the far right-hand side of the road. There are four types of design intended to make cycling safer: paved shoulders, cycling lanes, designated cycling routes, and bicycle paths.

Paved shoulders, marked off with a solid white line, allow cyclists to ride in the direction of traffic, alongside motor vehicles.

Cycling lanes in urban areas occupy part of the roadway, but are marked off or physically separated from traffic lanes and reserved exclusively for cyclists.

Designated cycling routes are usually found where motor vehicle traffic is light and slow moving; there are no protected corridors, merely signs.

Bicycle paths are designed exclusively for the use of cyclists, often away from motor vehicle traffic.

As for motor vehicles, signs for cyclists come in four types: regulatory, warning, work site and information signs.

NB The signs presented in this section do not appear in any other section.

Regulatory signs

Bicycle tab

Draws the attention of cyclists to any regulatory sign concerning them only.

Mandatory route

Indicates the route cyclists must take.

Indicate to cyclists and pedestrians the respective side they must use.

Indicates to cyclists and pedestrians they must share that portion of the way, there being no exclusive corridor for either.

Bicycle riders must dismount

Indicates to cyclists that they must dismount and walk beside their bicycle.

SIGNS FOR CYCLISTS

SIGNS FOR CYCLISTS

Children must ride with an adult

Indicates to cyclists under age 12 that they must be in the company of an adult in order to ride on a public roadway where the posted speed limit is over 50 km/h.

No passing

Indicates to cyclists that they cannot ride side-by-side; marks the start of a no-passing zone.

Indicates the end of a no-passing zone.

Bicycle symbol at a pedestrian light

Indicates to cyclists that they must cross on the walk signal.

Warning signs

Steep slope

Indicates the slope in percentage terms (at least 6%, which means a rise or drop of 6 m over 100 m).

Busy public access

Indicates to cyclists that a nearby public access entails the presence of motor vehicles.

Cyclists ahead

Bicycles crossing road nearby.

Indicates the presence of cyclists on a paved shoulder, over the distance shown, when it is placed below the bicycle sign.

Slippery surface

Warns that the road surface may be slippery in some places.

Work site signs

Cycle lane closed

Indicates that a cycle lane is temporarily closed.

Detour

Indicates to cyclists the direction of a detour because of road work.

Information signs

Indicates the direction to a bikeway

Directs cyclists to a bikeway.

Direction

Indicate the direction and distance in km to a destination by bicycle and facilities available. In cases where cyclists must share the route with pedestrians, a human silhouette is shown on this sign.

SIGNS FOR CYCLISTS

Bicycle route

Indicate the name and direction of a cycle lane or path.

Parking area for bicycles

Indicates the direction to parking for bicycles.

Parking area for cycling lane connection

Indicates where motor vehicle parking area provides access to a cycling lane or path.

Route verte identification

Indicates those parts of the trail where a bicycle may be used.

The *Route verte* is a bicycle trail more than 4,000 km long that stretches north to south, east to west, throughout the province. Comprised of off-road paths, paved shoulders and sections of small, quiet roads, it will eventually link 350 municipalities in 15 regions (where some four million Quebecers live). Clearly marked and very safe, the Route verte is a way to discover Quebec in all its greenery.

Beginning

Indicates the beginning of a bikeway.

Period when closed

SIGNS FOR CYCLISTS

Indicates the time of the year when the cycle path cannot be used.

Private tourist facilities

Indicates the attractions and services available to cyclists.

Commercial services

Indicate food and bicycle repair services located near a bicycle path.

Public services

Indicate services available along a bikeway.

Shelter

Heated shelter

Tourist information office

Drinking water

Rest area

Air pump

SIGNS FOR CYCLISTS

Telephone

Washroom

HIGHWAY SAFETY CODE PROVISIONS CONCERNING ROAD SIGNS AND TRAFFIC SIGNALS

Only the person responsible for maintaining a public highway may erect road signs or traffic signals, which must meet standards set by Transport Québec.

No person may:

- erect a signal, sign, indication or device on a public highway without the permission of the person responsible for the maintenance of that roadway;

- erect or display on private property a signal, sign, indication or device that encroaches on a public roadway or that could create confusion or obstruct any sign erected on a public roadway;

- travel on private property to avoid compliance with a road sign or traffic signal.

All persons must:

- comply with a road sign or traffic signal erected on a roadway under the *Highway Safety Code*;

- obey the orders or signals of a law enforcement officer, school crossing guard or flagperson in charge of directing traffic around a work site, even if contrary to existing traffic signals or signs.

Chapter 4

TRAFFIC RULES

The Highway Safety Code sets out the traffic rules for all users of public roadways, in particular motor vehicle operators. Pedestrians, motorcyclists, moped operators and cyclists also have certain rights and obligations when using a public roadway. For safety's sake, it is important to know these rules and follow them.

PROTECTION

SEAT BELT

Seat belts are not simply an accessory. They are an important safety feature that can save lives. Seat belt use is mandatory.

All occupants, except children whose sitting height is below 63 cm, as explained below, sitting on the front or back seat of a moving motor vehicle must wear the seat belt provided; this seat belt must be properly fastened. Driving a vehicle is prohibited if:

- the driver or passenger seat belt is missing or unusable or has been altered;
- a passenger under age 16 is not wearing a properly fastened seat belt.

A child whose sitting position measured to the top of the head comes below 63 cm must be seated in a restraint system or booster seat in compliance with regulations referred to in the *Motor Vehicle Safety Act.* The restraint system and booster seat must be adapted to the weight and size of the child, in accordance with the manufacturer's instructions, and must be properly installed in the vehicle. This obligation does not apply in taxis, in which case the child must be restrained by the seat belt available.

The Société de l'assurance automobile du Québec may, however, issue a certificate exempting a person, for exceptional medical reasons, from the obligation to wear a seat belt or the use of a restraint device.

Taxi drivers operating a vehicle as part of their job on a public roadway with a speed limit set by a municipality, or on an unnumbered roadway, are also exempt from the obligation to wear a seat belt.

Drivers are not required to wear a seat belt when backing up.

AIR BAG

Air bags are proven safety devices designed to prevent the occupants of a vehicle from striking their head, neck or chest against the instrument panel, steering wheel or windshield in a front-end collision. They also provide effective protection against potentially fatal injuries or injuries that may result in disability. Research in 1998 showed that the combined use of air bags and seat belts reduces the risk of severe head injury by 75% and severe chest injury by 66%.

Air bags are not designed to deploy in rear-end collisions, rollover accidents or in most side-on collisions.

Air bags contain tiny holes, which enable them to deflate upon absorbing the momentum from the occupant, thereby allowing the occupant to breathe and move.

Some measures can be taken to reduce risks during air bag deployment:

- an infant must always be seated in a rear-facing infant safety seat that is secured in the back seat (centre if possible);
- children age 12 and under must always be seated in a child safety seat adapted to their weight and size that is secured in the back seat;
- always wear a seat belt;
- move the seat back to ensure that there is a distance of at least 25 cm between the centre of the air bag cover and the middle of the driver's chest area.

The Société de l'assurance automobile du Québec may authorize an air bag to be deactivated if one of the drivers of a vehicle or a passenger is at risk when an air bag deploys. An application, however, must first be filed with the Société by completing the form entitled *Declaration of Requirement for Air Bag Deactivatiod*.

HEADREST

Thousands of Quebecers suffer whiplash in automobile accidents each year. Scarcely 10% of motorists in the province adjust their vehicle's headrest properly; the mistake the remainder make is placing it too low.

If the headrest is placed too low, behind the neck, it is of little use because in the event of a rear-end collision, the head will be thrust back, causing a neck injury.

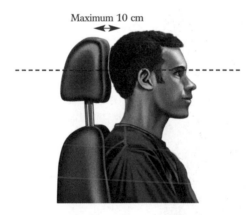

Maximum 10 cm

To offer adequate protection:
- the headrest must not be more than ten centimetres (10 cm) from the back of the head;
- the middle of the headrest must be level with the eyes or top of the ears.

TRAFFIC RULES

Whether turning, changing lanes, passing or carrying out another manoeuvre, motor vehicle operators must apply special rules in each case.

TRAFFIC LANE DIVISION

Some lines separating traffic lanes may be crossed, others may not.

Drivers may cross a **broken line** after ensuring that they can do so safely.

A **broken line next to a solid line** means passing is allowed if the broken line is on the vehicle's side when the manoeuvre is begun. Passing must be completed before the broken line ends.

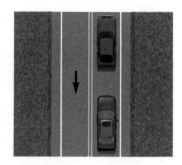

A **solid single line** or **solid double line** may not ordinarily be crossed.

However, these lines may be crossed if the traffic lane is obstructed or closed, or to make a left turn onto another roadway or into a private driveway. They can also be crossed to pass farm machinery, farm tractors, animal-drawn vehicles, bicycles or vehicles with a slow-moving vehicle warning sign (orange triangle with reflectorized red edges).

LANE USE

TWO-WAY TRAFFIC

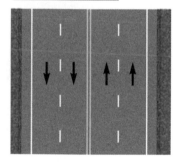

When travelling on a roadway similar to the one illustrated, motor vehicle operators must use the right-hand lane. They may use the left lane, however, to pass another vehicle or to avoid an obstacle. In both cases, drivers must make sure the left lane is free before entering it.

THREE OR FIVE LANES OF TWO-WAY TRAFFIC

When using a roadway divided into three or five lanes where there is traffic in both directions, motor vehicle operators must use the lane or lanes to the right. The centre lane is reserved for left turns by vehicles traveling in either direction.

LANE CLOSED

If one or more lanes in the direction the vehicle is travelling are closed or obstructed, the driver may use the nearest free lane intended for oncoming traffic, after yielding the right of way to any vehicle in that lane.

TWO OR THREE LANES FOR ONE-WAY TRAFFIC

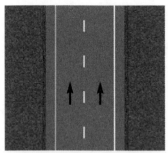

Drivers must in general keep to the far right when there are two lanes for traffic in the same direction.

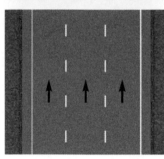

Generally speaking, when there are three lanes, drivers should use one of the right-hand lanes.

Particular circumstances:

- A motor vehicle operator may use the far left lane on an expressway to pass other vehicles, turn left, avoid obstacles, or move toward an exit lane.

- Slowing down in the left-hand lane is permitted, as long as the motor vehicle operator signals his/her intention to turn left or stop on the left side of the lane.

- Where the speed limit is not over 80 km/h, for instance on an urban boulevard, a motor vehicle operator may use either lane. Travelling faster than a vehicle in another lane is not considered passing.

ROADWAY SEPARATED BY A MEDIAN OR OTHER DIVIDER

Drivers must not cross medians or other dividers separating traffic lanes, except in those places indicated by the appropriate signs.

FREEWAY ACCESS AND EXIT RAMPS

To enter or exit a freeway, motor vehicle operators must use designated access and exit lanes.

SPEED LIMITS AND DISTANCE BETWEEN VEHICLES

Any act or speed likely to endanger people's lives or personal property is prohibited. These obligations apply on all public roadways and on private roadways open to public road vehicle traffic, as well as shopping centre parking lots and other areas open to public traffic.

Motor vehicle operators must respect the following speed limits:

- on freeways:
  - 60 km/h minimum;
  - 100 km/h maximum.

- on highways with a concrete or asphalt surface:
  - 90 km/h maximum.

- on gravel roads:
  - 70 km/h maximum.

- in a school zone when children are entering or leaving school:
  - 50 km/h maximum unless a sign indicates a different speed, which the driver must then obey.

- in cities, towns or villages, unless otherwise indicated:
  - 50 km/h maximum.

Drivers must reduce speed when travelling after dark, in fog, rain, snow and other conditions limiting visibility, as well as on a road surface that is slippery or not entirely cleared. They must also slow down when approaching road construction.

Drivers may not travel so slowly as to hinder the flow of traffic.

DISTANCE BETWEEN VEHICLES

When travelling behind another vehicle, motor vehicle operators must keep at a reasonable, safe distance from the vehicle ahead so that they can stop their vehicle without causing an accident should they need to stop quickly. Drivers must take into account traffic speed, traffic density, weather conditions and the state of the road surface. The "2-second" rule can be used to estimate the distance between two vehicles. This rule is described and illustrated in driving technique publications: *Driving a Passenger Vehicle; Operating a Motorcycle; Operating a Moped or Scooter.*

Motor vehicle operators travelling in a convoy on a public highway where the maximum speed is 70 km/h or higher must leave sufficient space between their vehicles. They must also allow other motor vehicle operators to pass them.

PASSING

Certain situations may call for passing another vehicle. Motor vehicle operators must follow certain rules when passing another vehicle.

Before passing another vehicle, drivers must:

- make sure passing is allowed (broken lines between lanes);
- make sure that the left lane is free and that no other vehicle coming from behind is going to occupy that lane;
- make sure that the lane they wish to enter is unoccupied for a sufficient distance;
- signal their intention to pass using turn-signal lights.

Passing should be avoided when travelling in fog or conditions that affect visibility.

Motor vehicle operators must use the left lane to pass. A passing vehicle must return to the right-hand lane once the manoeuvre is complete.

PASSING A BICYCLE

Motor vehicle operators wishing to pass a bicycle may remain in the same lane if there is enough room to complete the manoeuvre safely. The left lane may also be used.

BEING PASSED

Motor vehicle operators being passed or about to be passed by another vehicle must not accelerate. They may slow down out of courtesy, however, in order to facilitate the manoeuvre.

PASSING PROHIBITED

When motor vehicle operators need to use a lane reserved for oncoming traffic in order to pass, they must avoid doing so:

- when approaching or on top of a hill;
- in a curve;
- when approaching or crossing a marked pedestrian crosswalk, a level crossing or a tunnel;
- any other place where signs or pavement markings indicate that passing is prohibited.

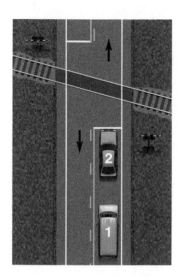
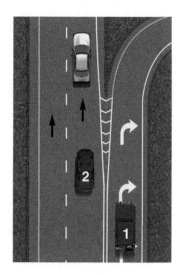

Vehicle 1 may not pass vehicle 2 in these situations.

Passing is also prohibited when there are vehicles in the left lane, or if a vehicle behind has signaled the intention to pass, or has begun to do so. In situations like those illustrated below, the driver of vehicle 1 must not pass.

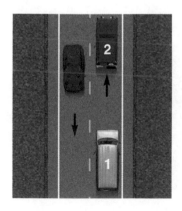
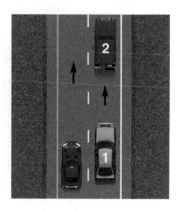

When driving on a roadway with two or more lanes of one-way traffic, motor vehicle operators must avoid:

- lane hopping;
- passing on the right, except:
    - when passing a vehicle making a left turn or heading toward an freeway exit ramp;
    - when passing a vehicle performing maintenance in the left lane.

At no time may a passing vehicle leave the roadway (e.g. drive on the shoulder) to perform the manoeuvre.

••• Passing in a slow lane •••

When there are slow lane signs, drivers travelling slowly must use the far right-hand lane. Slow lanes, created in order to maintain traffic flow, are usually found in mountainous regions. Any vehicle can use them – not just trucks.

Since some of these lanes are longer than 2 km, a broken line may be used over a certain distance to allow vehicles driving downhill to pass other vehicles.

Drivers in the slow lane on the far right may not return to the main lane when the roadway shows these markings.

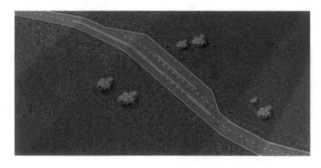

TURNING

Before turning at an intersection, motor vehicle operators must:

- make sure the turn can be completed safely;
- signal their intention to turn using the vehicle's turn-signal lights;
- yield the right of way to pedestrians or cyclists crossing the roadway they wish to enter;
- yield the right of way to vehicles travelling on the intersecting roadway, oncoming vehicles, or vehicles approaching or already in the intersection.

The driver then makes the turn when the coast is clear.

If the motor vehicle operator is unable to move into the designated turning lane when preparing to make a turn, he/she must make the turn at another intersection.

The following illustrations show the rules to follow when making the most common right and left turns.

RIGHT TURN

Motor vehicle operators planning to make a right turn onto a roadway with one or more lanes, whether for one- or two-way traffic, must:

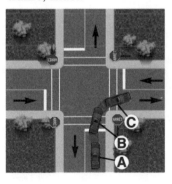

A. move to the far right-hand side of the roadway or to the lane designated for turning right;

B. advance in a straight line to the point where the two roads meet;

C. turn sharply and enter the far right-hand lane of the other roadway without encroaching upon the left lane or any bicycle lane or reserved lane.

LEFT TURN

At the intersection of roadways with traffic in both directions, motor vehicle operators planning to make a left turn must:

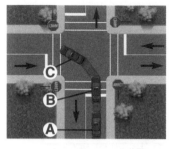

A. move over to the left lane or a turn lane of the road on which they are travelling;

B. advance in a straight line to the point where the two roads meet;

C. as soon as the coast is clear, turn into the nearest lane (furthest to the left) allowing travel in the desired direction.

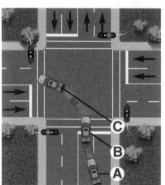

A. move over to the left lane or a turn lane of the road on which they are travelling;

B. advance in a straight line to the point where the two roads meet;

C. as soon as the coast is clear, turn into the nearest lane (furthest to the left) allowing them to travel in the desired direction.

When turning from a road with traffic in both directions onto a one-way road, drivers must:

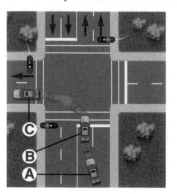

A. move over to the left lane or a turn lane of the road on which they are travelling;

B. advance in a straight line to the point where the two roads meet;

C. as soon as the coast is clear, enter the far left lane of the other roadway.

When turning from a one-way road onto a road with traffic in both directions, drivers must:

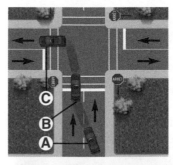

A. move over to the far left-hand lane or any other designated turning lane;

B. advance in a straight line to the point where the two roads meet;

C. enter the nearest lane (furthest to the left) allowing travel in the desired direction.

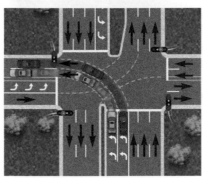

If there are two designated turning lanes, the turn should be completed in the corresponding lane of the other roadway.

When turning from a one-way road onto another one-way road, drivers must:

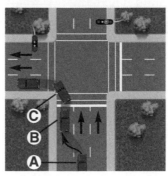

A. move over to the far left-hand lane or any other designated turning lane;

B. advance in a straight line to the point where the two roads meet;

C. enter the far left-hand lane of the other roadway.

AT AN INTERSECTION WHERE SEVERAL
VEHICLES ARE TURNING AT THE SAME TIME

At an intersection of two roads with more than one lane in both directions, when these manoeuvres are performed simultaneously by several vehicles, each driver must direct his/her vehicle into the correct lane.

Vehicles turning right must:

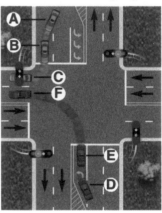

A. move into the lane on the extreme right or into a lane reserved for making turns;

B. advance in a straight line to the point where the two roads meet;

C. enter the far right-hand lane, without encroaching on the left lane, and respect reserved lanes or bicycle lanes.

Vehicles turning left must:

D. move into the left lane or into a lane reserved for making turns;

E. advance in a straight line to the point where the two roads meet;

F. enter the far left-hand lane, without encroaching on the right lane, as soon as the coast is clear.

Vehicles turning right on a red light

To safely right turn at a red light a driver must:

1. Stop:

> – at the approach of a red light, come to a complete stop at the stop line or in front of the pedestrian crossing.

2. Look:

> – check for a sign prohibiting right turns at a red light;
>
> – if there is no such sign, or outside of the time period indicated on the tab of a traffic light indicating that turning is prohibited, or outside the island of Montréal, ensure that no pedestrian is crossing or preparing to cross the intersection:
>
>> - yield the right of way to pedestrians and cyclists in the intersection or about to enter it. Pedestrians always have the right of way when facing a green traffic light or a pedestrian light allowing them to cross;
>>
>> - look left, ahead and right (mirror and blind spot) and a last time on the left;
>>
>> - yield to vehicles so as to not impede traffic;
>
> – be extra careful in the presence of children, the elderly, people with reduced mobility or anyone crossing slowly.

3. Decide:

> – turning right on a red light is not mandatory. It should be done only if the coast is clear.

INDICATING YOUR INTENTIONS AND PRESENCE

Indicating your intentions

Before changing lanes, making a U-turn (unless prohibited by a road sign), passing, making a turn or entering a roadway from the shoulder or a parking area, drivers must indicate their intentions using the vehicle's turn-signal lights continuously over a sufficient distance to ensure the operator's safety and that of other road users.

USING EMERGENCY FLASHERS

Motor vehicle operators who have to drive very slowly must use the vehicle's emergency flashers. Emergency flashers should be used only for reasons of safety (a breakdown or stalled vehicle on the roadway at night, for example).

USING HEADLIGHTS AND RUNNING LIGHTS

At night or in poor weather conditions, motor vehicle operators must ensure that headlights and running lights are on.

At night, drivers must switch from high beams to low beams:

- when coming within 150 m of an oncoming vehicle;
- when coming within 150 m of the vehicle ahead;
- when the roadway is well-lit.

YIELDING THE RIGHT OF WAY

The *Highway Safety Code* describes many situations where road users must yield the right of way.

PEDESTRIANS

Motor vehicle operators and cyclists must yield the right of way to pedestrians crossing or preparing to cross:

- at a green light;
- at a white pedestrian light, flashing or not;
- a pedestrian crosswalk;
- at an intersection with one or more stop signs;
- at an intersection with a yield sign.

YIELD SIGNS

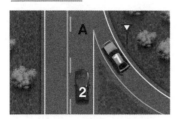

The driver of vehicle 1 must yield the right of way to vehicle 2 before entering lane A.

ENTERING AN FREEWAY

The driver of vehicle 1, when merging with the flow of traffic on the freeway, must yield the right of way to vehicle 2. In the example illustrated, this driver must pull in behind vehicle 2.

The driver of vehicle 2 must consider that a vehicle is trying to merge with traffic on the freeway and should change lanes if possible.

AT A MANDATORY STOP

At an intersection controlled by **a stop sign** on one roadway:

Drivers and cyclists required to stop at an intersection or flashing red light must yield the right of way to any vehicle on the other roadway already in the intersection or near enough to the intersection that entering it would be dangerous.

At **a four-way stop**:

Drivers or cyclists required to stop at the intersection must yield the right of way to any vehicle that reaches the intersection before them.

In both of these cases, the driver or cyclist must also yield the right of way to pedestrians or cyclists crossing the road that the driver or cyclist is about to cross or enter.

CERTAIN TRAFFIC LIGHTS

Motor vehicle operators or cyclists at any of the following traffic lights:

- flashing red light
- flashing yellow light
- green light, flashing or not
- green arrow

must yield the right of way to vehicles, cyclists and pedestrians already in the intersection or make sure that they can make it across the intersection safely.

WHEN TURNING AT AN INTERSECTION

Motor vehicle operators and cyclists must:

- Yield the right of way to pedestrians and cyclists crossing the roadway that they wish to enter. In the example illustrated, the driver of vehicle 1 yields the right of way to the pedestrian.

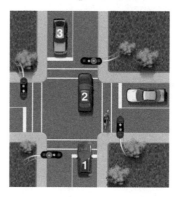

- Yield the right of way, when making a left turn, to any oncoming vehicle. In the example illustrated, vehicle 3 yields the right of way to vehicle 2, the pedestrian and vehicle 1.

ENTERING OR EXITING PRIVATE PROPERTY

Motor vehicle operators and cyclists wishing to enter or exit private property must yield the right of way to any vehicle or pedestrian travelling on a public roadway.

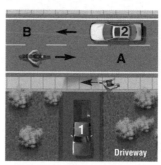

In this illustration, before entering lane A, the driver of vehicle 1 must yield the right of way to the pedestrian and motorcyclist.

Before entering lane B, the driver of vehicle 1 must yield the right of way to the pedestrian, motorcyclist and vehicle 2.

In the situation illustrated here, the driver must yield the right of way to the motorcyclist and pedestrian before entering the private driveway.

EMERGENCY VEHICLES

Motor vehicle operators and cyclists must allow unhindered passage for emergency vehicles with their lights flashing or siren in operation. This means reducing speed, keeping as far to the right as possible and stopping, thereby lessening the number of obstacles an emergency vehicle driver must contend with. It is very important to stay calm and to provide a free lane for emergency vehicles to pass, whether they are coming from behind or in the opposite direction. Stay clear of intersections and avoid turning in front of an emergency vehicle (turn farther on and backtrack, if necessary).In this way we can all help save lives. Seconds count: think about it!

BUSES

On public roads with a maximum speed limit under 70 km/h, motor vehicle operators must yield the right of way to a bus whose driver wishes to re-enter the lane the bus occupied before stopping. The bus driver must make sure that it is safe to do so, however, and indicate intentions using the turn-signal lights. This obligation only applies to drivers of vehicles in the lane that the bus driver wishes to re-enter.

SCHOOL BUSES

Motor vehicle operators must be ready to stop in the proximity of a school bus.

School buses make frequent stops to take on and drop off children. To avoid having other vehicles suddenly slow down or stop, the school bus driver who intends to stop must warn other vehicle operators, using the flashing amber lights.

Other drivers must be aware of these two stages:

- when the flashing amber lights or hazard lights of the bus are activated, other drivers **must prepare to stop**.
- when the flashing red lights of the bus are in operation or its stop arm extended, other drivers must bring their vehicle to a **full stop**.

Motor vehicle operators must stop at least five metres from a vehicle used to carry school children if it has its flashing red lights in operation or its mandatory stop arm extended. Drivers may pass the vehicle in either direction if its flashing red lights are off and the stop arm retracted, provided it is safe to do so. This applies to vehicles on the same roadway as a school bus, travelling in either direction.

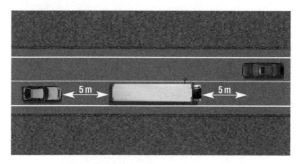

If the traffic lanes are separated by a median or another divider, however, oncoming vehicles are not required to stop.

LEVEL CROSSINGS

Motor vehicle operators and cyclists are required to stop at least five metres from a railway crossing if the arrival of a rail vehicle is indicated by flashing red lights, a lowered barrier, or a railway employee.

Drivers must not enter a level crossing if there is not enough free space ahead to clear the crossing completely.

Unless otherwise indicated, the driver of a bus, minibus or vehicle carrying hazardous material must stop at least five metres from a level crossing. Drivers may continue only when they are certain they can cross safely.

DRIVING IN REVERSE

When backing up, drivers must make sure the manoeuvre can be performed safely and without impeding traffic.

Driving in reverse is prohibited on freeways and on their access and exit ramps.

SHARING THE ROAD WITH HEAVY VEHICLES

Car, motorcycle and truck drivers have their own reasons for using the roadway. Each is required to behave responsibly. Here are a few safety rules that call for courtesy and tolerance when sharing the road with other users.

It is important to be aware of the limitations of driving a heavy vehicle in order to have a better understanding of the manoeuvres required of truck drivers and to drive defensively. Since trucks are longer, wider and heavier than other vchicles, they are more difficult to handle and react more slowly.

For example, a truck requires greater time and distance to stop. So, drivers travelling in front of heavy vehicles must signal their intention to turn or change lanes well ahead of time. Sudden moves such as quickly cutting in front of a heavy vehicle must be avoided at all costs. Drivers must plan for the extra time and distance required before passing a truck.

When a truck driver signals a turn at an intersection, all other drivers must cooperate by remaining behind and allowing the heavy vehicle to complete its turn without getting in its way.

Given the length and height of their vehicles, truck drivers have difficulty seeing other road users. A truck driver has blind spots at the front, rear and side of the vehicle. For example, a car driver or motorcyclist who is travelling behind a truck and who does not see any of the truck's side mirrors, is too close and cannot be seen by the truck driver. Road users should therefore avoid driving alongside a heavy vehicle for long periods and if they must pass a heavy vehicle, they should take as little time as possible in doing so.

HEAVY VEHICLE BLIND SPOTS

Blind spots are those areas of the road that a heavy vehicle operator cannot see because of the vehicle's size and design. Other road users should stay out of those areas because the risk of collision is higher. A heavy vehicle's blind spots are at the front, rear and sides.

FIVE TYPICAL SITUATIONS

••• In front of a heavy vehicle •••

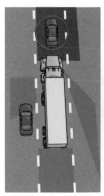 

A collision could occur where the driver of a light vehicle cuts quickly in front of a heavy truck, from the left or right lane and slows down once in front.

••• Behind a heavy vehicle •••

When the driver of a light vehicle follows close behind a heavy truck, which then stops or slows suddenly, the result could easily be an accident.

••• On either side of a heavy vehicle •••

There are blind spots on either side of a heavy vehicle, because these areas are not covered by the truck's rearview mirrors. A light vehicle in those blind spots could collide with the heavy vehicle, were it to move over to the left or to the right.

APPROACHING A ROAD WORK AREA

A series of orange diamond-shaped signs tell motorists that road work is being carried out further ahead. The work area may be identified by cones, barrels, barriers, signs, pavement markings, flashing arrows or signal lights.

Drivers must be particularly careful when nearing a work site:

- Remain patient. The purpose of road work is to improve traffic conditions. Some inconvenience to motorists therefore cannot be avoided.

- Obey all traffic signs, including the speed limit posted in road work areas, which carry the same penalties as normal posted speed limits.

- Reduce speed and maintain a greater distance from the vehicle ahead to allow enough time to react safely to the warning signs.

- Scan the road ahead and on the sides, and check the rearview mirrors frequently.

- Watch for site personnel, vehicles and equipment; they might appear unexpectedly.

- Exercise caution when coming to areas where the roadway narrows or lanes merge, which can create a funnel effect and slow traffic. Get into the open lane and remain there; waiting until the last moment before making a move is especially dangerous in work areas.

- Care is required when driving where temporary detours have been erected to divert traffic. Shoulders may also be lower than the road.

- Obey signal persons; their task is to direct traffic safely through work areas.

STOPPING AND PARKING

Just as vehicle movement is regulated, stopping is also subject to various rules:

OBLIGATIONS

Drivers must park their vehicles in the same direction as the flow of traffic and no more than 30 cm from the edge of the roadway. When parking on a grade, drivers must:

- engage the parking brake;
- turn the wheels to ensure that any movement of the vehicle's front will be made toward the nearest curb.

Drivers must not leave their vehicles without removing the key from the ignition and locking the doors. Also, no child under age 7 is to be left unattended in a vehicle.

Motorcycles, mopeds and motorized scooters may be parked diagonally to the edge of the nearest curb in the same direction as the flow of traffic.

Drivers who have to stop temporarily on the roadway at night must leave their running lights or their emergency flashers on. They may also signal the presence of the vehicle using lights or flares that are visible for a distance of at least 150 metres.

RESTRICTIONS

Only in cases of necessity may drivers stop or park their vehicles in such a way that they block a road sign, hinder traffic, road construction or maintenance work or block access to private property.

Parking or stopping is prohibited:

- any place where parking is forbidden by *no parking* signs;
- on a sidewalk or median;
- in or within five metres of an intersection, pedestrian crosswalk or level crossing;
- on a freeway or its access or exit ramps;
- on an elevated roadway, bridge or overpass or in a tunnel;
- on a public roadway where the speed limit is 70 km/h or over;
- within five metres of a stop sign, fire hydrant, police station or fire hall;
- in a traffic lane reserved for certain vehicles;
- within eight metres of a police station or fire hall located on the opposite side of the roadway;
- in zones reserved for buses, clearly identified as such;
- in loading zones;
- in front of a sidewalk access ramp for disabled persons;
- in a parking space reserved for disabled persons.

Despite the prohibitions, a driver may stop in these locations to take on or drop off a disabled person, where this can be done safely.

Nonetheless, to use a parking space reserved for the disabled, the vehicle must display a parking permit for that purpose.

Abandoning a vehicle on a public roadway is prohibited. Any vehicle abandoned on the roadway will be removed and placed in storage at the owner's expense.

SPACES RESERVED FOR DISABLED PERSONS
AND PARKING PERMITS

To use a parking space reserved for the disabled:

- the vehicle must display a parking permit issued by the Société de l'assurance automobile du Québec in the name of the driver or the person accompanying the disabled person;

- the parking permit must hang from the rearview mirror and be visible from the outside of the vehicle;

- the certificate issued by the SAAQ attesting that a permit has been issued must be in the driver or accompanying passenger's possession.

A parking space reserved for the disabled may also be used by someone who has a sticker, plate or permit displaying the international wheelchair symbol, issued by a Canadian jurisdiction outside Québec or a member country or associate member country of the European Conference of Ministers of Transport.

To qualify for a disabled parking permit, the person must meet the requirements of the Regulation respecting identification stickers for using parking spaces reserved for handicapped persons, that is be struck with a disability lasting at least six months that:

- results in a loss of independence;

- risks compromising the person's health and safety in movement between the parked vehicle and the destination.

To obtain one of these permits, the person must fill out the appropriate application form, submit it to the Société along with the required payment and, if applicable, provide at his/her expense a professional assessment demonstrating that the eligibility requirements are met.

A permit is issued to the disabled person and may not be loaned to anyone.

The SAAQ may also issue a permit to a public establishment as defined in the Act respecting health services and social services, if the establishment owns a vehicle equipped to carry wheelchair-bound passengers.

Where requested by a peace officer, the driver or passenger must immediately produce the certificate issued by the SAAQ attesting that a permit has been issued.

The SAAQ must be informed within 30 days of a change of address or the destruction or loss of a parking permit or related certificate.

The parking permit and certificate must be returned to the SAAQ if they are no longer used or if the conditions listed on the certificate no longer apply to the holder.

UNLAWFUL PRACTICES

DRIVING PROHIBITED - WHERE AND WHEN?

Certain manoeuvres and behaviour, whether or not a vehicle is stopped or in motion, are strictly prohibited or are restricted in order to ensure the safety of road users.

ON THE SHOULDER

Motor vehicle operators may not drive on the shoulder, except if necessary (lane closed or obstructed or emergency) or unless a sign indicates it is permitted.

EMERGENCIES

Motor vehicle operators must not operate vehicles when and where prohibited by the authorities because of an emergency, thaw, rain or flooding.

RACES OR RALLIES

Operating a motor vehicle for a wager or in a race with another vehicle is prohibited except in the case of a rally organized in accordance with established standards.

TOO MANY PASSENGERS

Motor vehicle operators may not carry more passengers than the amont of seating available in the vehicle.

No more than three people may sit on the front seat. If the vehicle has bucket seats, only two people may sit in the front.

No passengers may ride in the trailer or semi-trailer of a moving vehicle unless it is designed specifically for that purpose and the road used is closed to traffic.

ALCOHOL

Vehicle occupants are not allowed to drink alcohol while driving in traffic or while parked in an area where public traffic is permitted.

VEHICLE RESTRICTIONS

MOVING VEHICLES

Riding on, climbing up on and climbing down from the running board of a moving vehicle is prohibited. These practices are permitted only for people who, in the course of their work, must ride on a specially designed exterior portion of a vehicle.

The doors of a motor vehicle may be opened only if the vehicle is stationary and when doing so entails no danger.

LICENCE PLATE

Motor vehicle operators whose licence permits them to drive only on private property or private roads may not drive on a public roadway. However, operators of such vehicles, excluding vehicles with metal treads, may cross any public roadway other than a freeway.

SQUEALING TIRES

Squealing a vehicle's tires or stopping abruptly is prohibited unless necessary for reasons of safety.

Towing

Motor vehicle operators may not tow another vehicle whose wheels remain in contact with the ground, unless the vehicle is solidly secured by means of a bar.

Portable Music Players, Televisions and Radar Warning Devices

Motor vehicle operators may not wear a portable music player or headphones while driving.

Subject to the exceptions provided in the *Regulation respecting safety standards for road vehicles*, driving a motor vehicle equipped with any of the following is prohibited:

- a television or screen that displays information and is placed so that the driver can see the screen;
- a radar warning device.

Driving a motor vehicle is prohibited when a passenger, animal or object obstructs the driver's view.

RESTRICTIONS ON THE USE OF PUBLIC ROADWAYS

Objects and Obstacles

Generally speaking, throwing or dumping snow or ice on a pubic roadway is prohibited. It is also forbidden to throw any object whatsoever on the roadway or to put any obstacles in the way of traffic.

Animal Crossing

Farm animals may not be herded onto or across a public roadway unless accompanied by two people with red flags. They may not be herded at night and are not to be herded on a freeway under any circumstances.

Horseback Riding

It is forbidden to ride a horse on a freeway or its access or exit ramps, or anywhere else where prohibited by the appropriate signs.

SPECIAL RULES FOR CERTAIN USERS

The rules in this section apply specifically to certain categories of users and supplement the traffic rules already presented.

There may be regulations concerning other aspects of driving for the same categories of users, for example the *Regulation respecting road vehicles used for the transportation of school children*, the *Act respecting off-roadway vehicles* and a number of regulations that apply to heavy vehicle users. Therefore, it is necessary to refer to these regulations to find out what other obligations these users have.

PEDESTRIANS

MANDATORY IDENTIFICATION

As road users, pedestrians are now required to state their name and address or present their driver's licence when asked to do so by a law enforcement officer who believes that a *Highway Safety Code* offence has been committed.

OBLIGATIONS

If there is a sidewalk along a roadway, pedestrians must use it. In the absence of a sidewalk, pedestrians must face traffic and walk on the shoulder or along the edge of the roadway.

Pedestrians wishing to cross a public roadway must use any nearby pedestrian crosswalk or intersection, after ensuring it is safe to do so.

If there is no intersection or pedestrian crosswalk nearby, pedestrians crossing a public roadway must yield the right of way to cyclists and vehicles.

Pedestrians must observe the walk signals at an intersection. The white signal authorizes a pedestrian to cross, while a flashing signal indicates to pedestrians who have already started to cross that they should be quick to reach the sidewalk or median. An orange signal prohibits pedestrians from starting across the roadway.

Pedestrians must obey traffic lights if there are no pedestrian signals.

RESTRICTIONS

The *Highway Safety Code* also prohibits pedestrians from:

- crossing an intersection diagonally, unless a traffic sign or signal expressly allows them to do so;
- hitch-hiking by standing on the roadway or in a location where passing is prohibited;
- standing on the roadway to speak with the occupant of a road vehicle;
- walking along an freeway or its entrance or exit ramps, except if necessary. Pedestrians may cross such a road only at traffic lights;
- using skates, skis, a skateboard or a toy vehicle on the roadway.

SOME SAFETY TIPS

Before crossing, pedestrians should look over their shoulder to make sure that no vehicle is approaching from behind to turn onto the road they are crossing. Look left, then right and left again before starting across; also learn to correctly estimate the time needed to cross the road safely.

At night, wear brightly-coloured clothing. Reflector tape on clothing and school bags improves the visibility of children walking to and from school.

BICYCLES

Cycling as a means for transportation is an effective means of protecting the environment, improving health and reducing traffic congestion. Using a bicycle on the road, however, is not without its risks and each year many cyclists are accident victims.

Cyclists are subject to the same basic traffic rules as other road users, as well as certain additional provisions that apply to them alone. Furthermore, the *Highway Safety Code* requires that cyclists identify themselves to any police office who believes that an offence has been committed.

MANDATORY ACCESSORIES

Bicycles must be equipped with a white reflector in front and red reflectors at the rear and on the spokes of the rear wheel. They must also have amber reflectors on each pedal and on the spokes of the front wheel. Bicycles must be equipped with at least one white headlight and one red taillight for night riding.

A bicycle must be equipped with at least a rear-wheel braking system capable of blocking the wheel immediately.

CYCLING RULES

Cyclists must hold onto the handlebars at all times and ride in single file when travelling with anyone else or in a group, which may not include any more than 15 cyclists. Cyclists must ride on the far right-hand side of the roadway, in the same direction as traffic, except:

- when the way is blocked; or
- when preparing to turn left.

Not only must cyclists obey road signs and traffic lights, they must use hand signals in a continuous manner and over a sufficient distance to make their intention known to other road users:

| to slow down or stop, by holding the left forearm down at a right angle to the road | to turn right, by holding the left forearm up at a right angle to the road, or by holding the right arm out horizontally | to turn left, by holding the left arm out horizontally |

If the roadway includes a bike path or lane, cyclists must use it. Similarly, it is preferable to use the asphalt shoulder if the road has one.

Riding a bicycle is prohibited between two adjacent lanes of vehicles, whether the vehicles are stopped or moving, on freeways or on freeway exit or entrance ramps.

Cycling is prohibited on public roadways with a maximum speed limit over 50 km/h, unless:

- the road has a clearly indicated and physically separated bike lane;
- the cyclist is at least 12 years old; or
- the cyclist is taking part in an excursion supervised by an adult.

Drinking alcoholic beverages while cycling is forbidden, as is carrying a passenger on a bicycle that is not equipped with a fixed seat for that purpose. Cyclists are not to ride on the sidewalk unless they have to or unless permitted by the appropriate signs.

It is also forbidden for cyclists to hold onto a moving vehicle or to ride while using earphones or a portable music player.

FOR ADDED SAFETY

Wear light or brightly-coloured clothing when riding a bicycle, to make it easier for other road users to see you.

Although not compulsory, wearing a helmet provides effective protection from head injury in the event of a fall.

A pennant on an arm at the side of a bicycle will force motorists to leave more space between their vehicle and the bicycle when passing.

Using a basket or carrier if needed will increase safety.

Frequently check a bike's operating condition and its components and accessories – handlebars, wheels, rims, chain and brakes.

ELECTRIC BICYCLE

The rider of a power-assisted bicycle must:

- be at least age 14;
- wear a bike helmet;
- if between the ages of 14 through 17, hold a licence authorizing him/her to drive a moped or scooter.

Anyone age 18 or over does not require such a licence to ride a power-assisted bicycle.

Recent provisions of the *Highway Safety Code* also allow the rider of a power-assisted bicycle to chose to use a bikeway or the road, unlike a traditional cyclist who is required to use a bikeway where available on a public road.

The features of an electric power-assisted bicycle must comply with the provisions of the *Motor Vehicle Safety Act* and the *Highway Safety Code.* The bicycle must be designed to operate on two or three tires and must be equipped with pedals and an electric motor that does not exceed 500 watts of power, which ceases to generate power once the bicycle reaches a speed of 32 km/h.

A power-assisted bicycle cannot be used to pull another person.

FOOT SCOOTER

For improved road safety, use of a foot scooter on a public road is prohibited at night unless it is equipped with a white reflector or white reflective material at the front, red reflector or red reflective material at the rear and on each side near the back of the scooter. If a scooter is not equipped with reflectors, riders must wear reflective material on clothing or an accessory to be visible to road users at night. Failure to respect these conditions for use of a scooter at night is punishable by a $25 to $50 fine.

A foot scooter must be equipped with at least a rear-wheel braking system. The owner of a foot scooter that is not equipped with a braking system is liable to a fine of $15 to $30.

MOTORCYCLES, MOPEDS AND MOTORIZED SCOOTERS

Motorcycle, moped and scooter operators must remain seated and hold the handlebars when the vehicle is in operation. When riding, the white headlight must remain on at all times. Passengers must be seated facing the handlebars, with their feet on the footrests. When travelling in groups of two or more in a traffic lane, they must ride in staggered (zigzag) formation.

Riders must wear a helmet that meets safety standards. The same applies to rear or sidecar passengers. Operators and passengers are required to produce their helmets for inspection at the request of a law enforcement officer.

Riding a motorcycle, moped or scooter between two lines of vehicles in adjacent lanes, whether the vehicles are stopped or moving, is prohibited. What is more, the use of motorcycles, scooters or mopeds whose engine has a cylinder size of 125 cc or less is prohibited on freeways and on freeway access and exit ramps.

The operator of a motorcycle, scooter or moped may carry a passenger only if the vehicle is permanently equipped with a fixed seat for that purpose and footrests on either side.

Riding on a sidewalk is prohibited except if necessary or where permitted by the appropriate signs.

Motorcycle, scooter and moped operators must obey all road signs.

MAKE SURE YOU CAN BE SEEN

Motorcycles, scooters and mopeds must be equipped with at least one headlight in front, one red tail-light, two turn-signal lights at the front and rear and a red brake light. Sidecars must be equipped with a red light at the rear, located as far to the right as possible.

Since 80% to 90% of all the information which vehicle operators receive is through what they see, riders must constantly make sure that other road users can see them. This is why their headlight should remain on the entire time the vehicle is in operation. Another way to be seen is to remain in the proper lane position at all times and wear bright-coloured clothing with reflector strips at night.

EMERGENCY VEHICLES

Emergency vehicle operators should only activate flashing signal lights or sirens or any other accessory when needed for their job.

They are exempt from traffic rules concerning speed limits, passing, stopping and parking, road signs and traffic lights, and right of way.

VEHICLES USED TO CARRY SCHOOL CHILDREN

Drivers of buses or minibuses used to carry school children may not have more passengers than the number of available seats.

They may not set the vehicle in motion unless everyone is seated and must ensure that passengers remain seated throughout the trip.

Drivers of buses or minibuses used to carry school children must warn other road users that the vehicle has stopped to allow passengers to get on or off by using flashing lights and the stop arm until the passengers are safe. This means leaving the lights on and the retractable stop arm extended until the passengers have reached the sidewalk or roadside.

When a school bus driver is stopped in traffic behind another vehicle used to carry school children whose lights are flashing, he/she must activate the flashing lights and extend the stop arm as well. Under no other circumstances, aside from taking on or letting children get down, should the driver operate the flashing lights or extend the stop arm.

VEHICLES TRAVELLING ON LOGGING ROADS

Since April 1, 1999, certain sections of the *Highway Safety Code* apply on logging roads just as they do on all of Québec's public roadways.

No drinking and driving

Now, anyone suspected of driving on a logging road while impaired may be stopped by a law enforcement officer and submitted to a breathalyzer test.

Speed limit

A speed limit of 70 km/h must now be observed on logging roads, unless signs and signals indicate otherwise. It is also important to adjust speed in keeping with road conditions.

Furthermore, all drivers must carry with them a valid driver's licence for the appropriate class of vehicle, the vehicle's registration certificate and proof of liability insurance.

Seat belts buckled

On logging roads, the driver and passenger must wear their seat belts.

A vehicle in good working order

All vehicles travelling on logging roads must be in good working order. Their load must also be securely attached in compliance with the standards for securing loads set out in the *Highway Safety Code.*

Drive on the right

Logging roads are used by all sorts of vehicles: cars, vans, recreational vehicles, etc. However, they are especially used by trucks carrying heavy loads. Drivers must therefore be very careful at all times and always drive on the right-hand side of the road when meeting another vehicle – especially in curves and on slopes.

Driving safely on logging roads is a matter of common sense.

- Reduce your speed before crossing a bridge. There is often only one lane on a bridge.

- Park your vehicle on the side of the road so that it is visible but out of the way of traffic. Never park it in a curve or on a grade. The same rules apply when observing animals by the road.

- Use a CB radio to signal your position to other vehicles on the logging road.

- If you need to pass another vehicle, proceed at a moderate speed to avoid projecting gravel or stones up onto the vehicle's windshield.

- Be extra careful at the beginning and the end of the day, in order to avoid hitting an animal.

- Before you set out, make sure that you have two spare tires.

- Drive with your headlights on at all times.

LOADS

The *Highway Safety Code* requires drivers:

- to observe regulations concerning the transport of hazardous materials and to follow the instructions of a law enforcement officer who asks to inspect the cargo, providing the officer with any documents concerning the cargo, or that attest to one's qualifications for the hauling of hazardous material;

- to put a red flag or reflective panel on the back of a load extending more than one metre beyond the rear of the vehicle. If the vehicle is driven at night, it must be equipped with a red light visible at a distance of 150 metres from the rear and side;

- to equip any slow-moving vehicle with a warning sign.

The *Highway Safety Code* prohibits anyone from operating a vehicle or allowing a vehicle to be operated when the cargo:

- is not properly secured or covered so that none of its parts can move;

- reduces the driver's field of vision or covers the headlights or other lights;

- compromises the stability or handling of the vehicle.

The driver must not allow passengers in a trailer or semi-trailer in motion.

HEAVY VEHICLES

Drivers, owners and operators of heavy vehicles (road vehicles and combination road vehicles with a net weight of over 3,000 kg, buses, minibuses, tow trucks and road vehicles used to haul hazardous material) must abide by a number of special rules for heavy vehicles.[3]

PRE-TRIP INSPECTION

Drivers must make sure that their vehicle does not have any defects. So that they can drive safely, they must inspect their vehicle before they leave on a trip, noting their observations and the mechanical condition of the vehicle in their inspection report, and immediately report any mechanical defect to the operator. They must also fill out and update the inspection report daily for the heavy vehicle they drive and keep it on board the vehicle.

---

3 More information on heavy vehicles is contained in the guide "*Driving a Heavy Vehicle*" from Les Publications du Québec and in "Obligations of Heavy Vehicle Users", "Daily Pre-Trip Inspection Guide" other publications of the Société de l'assurance automobile du Québec

The heavy vehicle operator must put an inspection report form in the vehicle. The operator must make sure that the driver keeps this report in the cab of the heavy vehicle and enters all required information in it. The operator must also inform the owner of any defect noted and send the owner a copy of the heavy vehicle inspection report. The operator must not use a heavy vehicle that has a major defect.

The owner of the heavy vehicle must correct any mechanical defects reported to him/her. Minor defects must be repaired within 48 hours. If the vehicle has major defects, however, driving it is prohibited. The owner must also ensure that he/she obtains a copy of the inspection report when the heavy vehicle is used by the operator.

The inspection report must always be kept in the heavy vehicle. A missing report constitutes an offence.

DRIVING HOURS AND HOURS OF SERVICE

Drivers must observe the regulatory standards governing driving and duty time. They must keep a daily log of their hours and keep on board the vehicle the daily driving and duty time logs for preceding days, using the given reference period to calculate the authorized number of hours.

Operators must ensure that drivers enter the required information in the daily driving and duty time log and that they keep them in the heavy vehicle. Operators must also make sure that drivers respect the number of driving and duty hours and that drivers give them a copy of their daily logs upon their return.

DRIVER'S LICENCE

Heavy vehicle drivers must have a driver's licence corresponding to the type of vehicle used and including the appropriate endorsements, such as for a manual transmission, air brakes or a road train.

They must also inform the operator, owner or any person who provides driving services if their driver's licence is revoked or suspended and of any change of class qualifying them to drive the vehicle.

Drivers must also comply with the demands of a law enforcement officer who takes their driver's licence away because they have gone over the driving and duty time provided for by regulation for the period corresponding to the prescribed number of hours of rest.

OTHER OBLIGATIONS

Heavy vehicle drivers must pull into an inspection station on the orders of an authorized officer or signal. This requirement does not apply to drivers of an emergency vehicle responding to a call or returning to post.

They must not drive a vehicle where the load has not been placed, secured or covered in accordance with the *Regulation respecting standards for the securing of loads*, which sets forth standards based on the type of load carried.

Drivers must also ensure that the vehicle's length and width are within prescribed limits and that the load does not exceed norms.

Owners or lessors of oversized vehicles must obtain a special travel permit to operate them. Drivers must carry these permits with them when driving and abide by their conditions.

EXTRA RULES CONCERNING BUSES

When allowing passengers to get on or off a bus, drivers must stop the bus on the far right-hand side of the roadway or in areas set aside for this purpose, after ensuring that they can do so safely. Doors are not to be opened until the vehicle has reached a full stop.

Bus drivers must distribute baggage and freight properly in the bus.

School bus drivers must not take on more passengers than the amount of seating available. It should be pointed out that this rule does not apply to any other city or rural bus or a minibus used in or outside cities, provided that the number of passengers in excess of the amount of seating available is no more than one passenger per row of seats.

OVERSIGHT OF HEAVY VEHICLE USERS

In 1998, an oversight mechanism was created to evaluate the conduct of heavy vehicle users.

••• Registration •••

Since April 1999, heavy vehicle owners and operators have had to register with the Commission des transports du Québec.

••• Follow-up •••

A case file for evaluating the conduct of heavy vehicle users is created by the Société de l'assurance automobile du Québec. This file is based on offences committed on the road or within companies, on accidents in which users and their drivers are involved, and on mechanical inspection results.

••• Rating •••

As of 1999, all owners and operators of a heavy vehicle are given a conduct rating. These ratings make it possible to pinpoint heavy vehicle users who represent a roadway safety risk or a risk to the roadway system.

••• Penalties •••

Penalties directed at owners and operators of heavy vehicles are geared towards improving their roadway behaviour. They include activities designed to increase awareness and provide support, as well as highway and company monitoring. The file of a high-risk owner or operator may be referred to the Commission des transports du Québec, however, for the imposition of a penalty, in particular mandatory highway safety courses, for more frequent mechanical inspections, or for the installation of speed limiting devices.

SHARING THE ROAD AND HANDLING HEAVY VEHICLES

Defensive driving should be practised at all times, because the consequences of any accident involving a heavy vehicle are bound to be serious. Since many drivers are unaware of the limits of driving a heavy vehicle, they are not really in a position to anticipate truck drivers' manoeuvres.

As regular road users, truck drivers must help other drivers by signaling their intentions. To ensure that other drivers see them, they should, like other vehicles, drive with their headlights on. The use of reflector strips on trucks is recommended.

So that they do not slow down traffic, truck drivers should use the far right-hand lane if they are travelling more slowly. When there is a special lane reserved for slow-moving vehicles, they should use it.

Since a truck requires more time and a greater distance to stop than a car, truck drivers must never exceed the maximum load or the speed limit. They must ensure that their brakes are always in good working order. Truck drivers must also obey speed limits and be extra careful at night or in poor weather or poor road conditions. They must at all times avoid tailing anyone too closely.

OFF-ROAD VEHICLES

The following are considered to be off-road vehicles:

- snowmobiles with a net weight of 450 kg or less and a width, including accessories, of no more than 1.28 metres;
- all-terrain vehicles (ATVs) with handlebars and at least two wheels which can be straddled and whose net weight is no more than 600 kg;
- other motor vehicles intended for use off public roadways and provided for by regulation.

Off-road vehicles, ATVs and snowmobiles are very popular. Unfortunately, carelessness and a lack of proper safety equipment have resulted in serious injury and even death for many riders. Operators who do not follow the traffic rules governing these vehicles are breaking the law and are endangering their lives and the lives of those around them.

RULES FOR USING OFF-ROAD VEHICLES

The operator of an off-road vehicle must be at least 14 years old.

Those under age 16 must have a certificate from the Fédération des clubs de motoneigistes du Québec or the Fédération québécoise des clubs "quads" attesting that they have the skills and knowledge required to operate these vehicles.

In order to use a public roadway, drivers of off-road vehicles must have a licence that authorizes them, under the *Highway Safety Code,* to drive a road vehicle on a public roadway and must abide by its conditions and restrictions. Persons age 16 or over need to have a class 5 or 6 driver's licence or probationary licence (6A, 6B or 6C); those under 16 need a class 6D licence authorizing them to operate a moped or scooter.

Owners of off-road vehicles must take out a third-party liability insurance policy for at least $500,000 that guarantees compensation for bodily injury or property damage caused by the vehicle.

Drivers of off-road vehicles must carry with them the vehicle's registration certificate issued under the *Highway Safety Code,* proof of third-party liability insurance, proof of age and, if applicable, their qualification certificate or authorization to drive.

If the vehicle is leased or rented from a dealer for less than one year, they must also carry proof of the duration of the lease or a copy of the contract with the dealer.

No more passengers may be carried on an off-road vehicle than the number stipulated by the manufacturer.

If the manufacturer of the off-road vehicle does not specify the maximum number of passengers allowed on the vehicle, only one passenger may be carried on a snowmobile and no passengers may be carried on other off-road vehicles.

An extra passenger may be carried if the vehicle has accessories designed for this purpose and if it is installed in keeping with the standards of the manufacturer of the off-road vehicle.

Off-road vehicles are not allowed to tow any more than one sled or one trailer at a time.

Anyone travelling on an off-road vehicle or on a sled or a trailer pulled by an off-road vehicle must wear the following equipment, which must meet regulatory standards:

- a helmet;
- safety glasses if the helmet does not have a visor;
- any other equipment prescribed by regulation.

Drinking alcoholic beverages is prohibited on off-road vehicles and on sleds or trailers towed by off-road vehicles.

All off-road vehicles must be equipped with the following items, which must meet regulatory standards:

- a white headlight;
- one red parking light at the rear;
- an exhaust system;
- a brake system.

Furthermore, all off-road vehicles manufactured after January 1, 1998 must be equipped with:

- a red brake light at the rear;
- a rearview mirror that is securely attached to the left side of the vehicle;
- a speedometer.

Equipment installed by the manufacturer that is required for the operation of an off-road vehicle, sled or trailer must not be removed.

Any modification to the vehicle that is liable to decrease its stability or the effectiveness of its brakes or to increase its acceleration capability is prohibited.

TRAFFIC RULES FOR OFF-ROAD VEHICLES

Off-road vehicles are allowed to use private roads and roadways open to public road vehicles. The owner of the road or the person in charge of its maintenance may, however, place signs prohibiting use of the road or restricting its use to certain types of off-road vehicles or to certain times of the year.

Operating off-road vehicles is prohibited on a public roadway, as understood within the *Highway Safety Code.*

The driving of an off-road vehicle at a distance inferior to that stipulated under a municipal bylaw or, failing that, within 30 metres of a house, health facility or recreational, sports, cultural or educational area is prohibited unless:

- expressly authorized by the owner or tenant of the house or the special area;
- on a public roadway under the conditions provided for by the *Act respecting off-highway vehicles*;
- on a private road open to public road vehicle traffic;
- on a trail created along a disused railway right-of-way and shown on the development plan of a regional county municipality or an urban community.

Off-road vehicles may however:

- be used on a road for a maximum distance of 1 km, if the driver is a worker who requires use of the vehicle to perform his/her work, provided that the worker observes highway traffic rules;
- cross a roadway at right angles, on the condition that a road sign indicates a crossing for off-road vehicles;

- be used off a road and outside of a ditch, even in the opposite direction, subject to conditions defined by regulation;
- be taken on the road for a maximum distance of 500 metres in order to reach a trail, service station or another place open to the public, where authorized by a road sign;
- travel on a road where road traffic is closed because of a special event or due to weather conditions, with the authorization of the person in charge of maintaining the road and on the conditions determined by that person;
- travel on all or part of a roadway that a government department or municipality is in charge of maintaining as determined by regulation or bylaw, and subject to the conditions, time of day and type of vehicle specified in the regulation or bylaw, provided the driver abides by the rules of the road.

Drivers of off-road vehicles must abide by road signs and traffic signals and obey the orders and signals of a law enforcement officer or trail supervisor.

The maximum speed limit for snowmobiles is 70 km/h and the speed limit for other off-road vehicles is 50 km/h.

Drivers of off-road vehicles must keep their white headlight and their red taillight on.

No one can travel on a trail unless they are on an off-road vehicle authorized for use on the trail. Drivers of off-road vehicles must keep to the right of a trail.

Chapter 5

ACCIDENTS

*S*ome 200,000 accidents occur each year in
Québec, with victims numbering in the tens of
thousands. They are entitled to compensation under
our public automobile insurance plan, which covers
all Québec residents and provides compensation
for bodily injury regardless of where an accident
occurs or who is at fault.

Coverage may also extend to non-residents for
injuries sustained in a road mishap in Québec.

AUTOMOBILE INSURANCE

IN QUÉBEC

Every vehicle owner must remember that:

- he/she is required, under the
Automobile Insurance Act, to
hold a third-party liability
insurance contract covering
property damage for a minimum amount of $50,000.
This type of coverage is available from private insurers;

- the Société de l'assurance automobile du Québec com-
pensates, regardless of fault, all Quebecers who suffer
bodily injury in a road accident occurring inside or
outside Québec, whether they be:
  - automobile drivers and passengers;
  - motorcycle riders;
  - cyclists and pedestrians (if struck by a motor vehicle).

The public insurance plan, which has been in effect since 1978, protects all Québec residents. It is a no-fault insurance plan, which means that accident victims do not have to wait for blame to be established before receiving compensation for bodily injury. Remedy through the courts has accordingly been abolished.

People will still be prosecuted, of course, for dangerous driving and related offences under the *Highway Safety Code* or the *Criminal Code*.

OUTSIDE QUÉBEC

All Quebecers injured in an accident outside the province are entitled to the compensation for bodily injury that is provided for under the public automobile insurance plan, whether they are to blame or not.

However, a Quebecer responsible for an accident outside Québec may be sued before the courts of the jurisdiction where the accident occurred for the bodily injury or property damage he/she caused. The driver is protected by third-party liability insurance taken out with a private insurer, mandatory for travel in North America. That coverage must be of sufficient amount to pay all compensation.

Before travelling in another Canadian province or in the United States, Quebecers should check with their private insurer to see that their liability insurance is sufficient to cover the bodily injury and property damage another party could sustain in the event of an accident. When driving a motor vehicle in other parts of the world, residents are also advised to find out how much coverage is necessary to be well-protected.

A Québec resident who is not at fault retains the right under the laws of that jurisdiction to sue for any amount of compensation in excess of what the Société pays.

NON-RESIDENTS

People whose permanent residence is located outside Québec are covered by the public insurance plan as the owner, operator or passenger of a motor vehicle registered in Québec. Such non-residents are entitled to the same benefits as a Quebecer if they become involved in an accident on Québec roads.

Other non-residents involved in an automobile accident in Québec are compensated by the Société to the extent that they are not responsible for the accident (inverse proportion to fault). Agreements have been reached with Ontario, Manitoba and Alberta under which their residents are compensated by their own insurer according to the principles and rates of the Québec plan regardless of fault.

TYPES OF ACCIDENT EXCLUDED

Some types of accident are not covered by the public plan and the persons involved are not entitled to compensation.

Such is the case of:

- an accident that occurs in an automobile race, contest or show, whether as drivers, passengers or spectators;
- an accident involving a snowmobile or other vehicle intended for off-road use, unless the collision involves a moving motor vehicle authorized to travel on a public roadway (e.g: car/snowmobile crash);
- an accident involving an equipment vehicle or trailer (e.g: snow removal vehicle) or a farm tractor, unless the collision involves a moving motor vehicle authorized to travel on a public roadway (e.g: car/tractor crash);
- bodily injury caused by equipment that can function independently from the vehicle of which it is part (e.g: a snow plow installed temporarily on a truck) when that vehicle is stopped on a public roadway, or on a private road, stopped or in motion.

To be protected in the latter three cases, the vehicle or equipment owner must take out appropriate coverage with a private insurer for any bodily injury and property damage that might be caused by his/her vehicle or equipment.

SPECIAL CASES

On-the-job automobile accidents

Any claim for compensation in connection with automobile accidents that occur on the job must be submitted to the Commission de la santé et de la sécurité du travail (CSST).

A claimant who has been turned down by the CSST may then file a claim for compensation with the Société, enclosing the letter of rejection from the CSST.

Victims of criminal acts; persons injured while assisting someone in distress

The victim of an assault in which an automobile caused injury has the option of being compensated under the *Crime Victims Compensation Act* or the *Automobile Insurance Act*.

A person injured by an automobile while assisting someone in distress may elect compensation under the *Act to promote good citizenship* or the *Automobile Insurance Act*.

A person who chooses to be compensated under either the *Crime Victims Compensation Act* or the *Act to promote good citizenship* must contact the nearest CSST regional office.

COMPENSATION

The Société pays compensation in one or more of the following forms to the victims of bodily injury sustained in a motor vehicle accident:

- an income replacement indemnity;
- an indemnity for care expenses;
- a lump sum for aftereffects of injury, such as loss of enjoyment of life, pain and mental suffering;
- the reimbursement of certain expenses incurred due to the accident (e.g: medication, transport by ambulance, purchase of prostheses or orthopedic devices, replacement of damaged clothing, home care expenses, etc.);

- a lump-sum indemnity for the loss of an entire school year or a semester at the postsecondary level;
- a care allowance;
- reimbursement of substitute labour costs for persons working without pay in a family business;
- death benefits;
- a lump sum to cover funeral costs.

Most indemnities paid by the Société are indexed yearly on January 1.

The Société is authorized to take the steps necessary for a victim's rehabilitation and his or her return to normal life as well as reintegration into the working world. For instance, the Société may cover the cost of alterations to a home or vehicle, the purchase of special equipment and job training or labour market reintegration if it considers these essential to the rehabilitation of an accident victim.

RIGHT OF CHALLENGE

A person who is dissatisfied with a decision rendered by a Société compensation officer may ask for a review of the case in writing within 60 days of the postmark date of the compensation officer's decision. The application must be submitted to the Société's review office on the *Application for Review* form before the end of the allotted time. It must set forth the reasons for wanting a review, and include supporting documents where possible. The application form must be signed by the claimant.

A person who remains dissatisfied following the Société's review decision is entitled to contest it within 60 days before the Administrative Tribunal of Québec, whose decision is final.

PROPERTY DAMAGE

Liability insurance for property damage to another party in a road accident is compulsory in Québec. When a collision occurs between at least two vehicles, the owners of which are known, each owner must file a claim with his/her own insurer (Direct Compensation Agreement).

HIT-AND-RUN AND INSOLVENCY

Some accident victims who sustain property damage find themselves without coverage when faced with insolvency on the part of the person responsible for the accident, or in a hit-and-run situation. The Société de l'assurance automobile du Québec may, in certain cases, compensate such victims for bodily injury and property damage sustained in the accident.

ACCIDENTS INVOLVING PROPERTY DAMAGE

Someone who sustained damage to their vehicle or to other property in an automobile accident may be compensated:

- if a Québec court has handed down a decision in his or her favour which cannot be satisfied because the party responsible for the accident is insolvent or did not have sufficient liability insurance coverage;
- the identity of the operator or owner of the vehicle that caused the accident is not known (hit-and-run).

Victims of a motor vehicle accident which did not occur on a public roadway and was caused by a farm tractor or trailer, a snowmobile, an equipment vehicle or trailer, or any vehicle not meant to be operated on a public roadway, may apply to the Société for compensation of bodily injury and property damage:

- when a Québec court has handed down a decision in their favour which cannot be satisfied because the party responsible for the accident is insolvent or did not have sufficient liability insurance coverage;

- the identity of the operator or owner of the vehicle that caused the accident is not known.

WHAT TO DO IN THE EVENT OF AN ACCIDENT

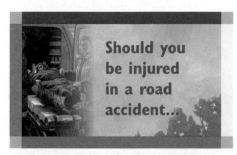

Should you
be injured
in a road
accident...

Call:
1 888 810-2525

The public plan administered by the
SAAQ covers all Quebecers injured in
a road accident wherever the mishap
occurs, regardless of fault.

For information or to claim
compensation, telephone
the Société de l'assurance
automobile du Québec.

Société de l'assurance
automobile
Québec

If INJURED in a motor vehicle accident:

- **Call the police to the scene so a report can be made of the accident;**
- **See a physician without delay and have all signs of injury entered on the doctor's report. Make sure the report is sent to the SAAQ;**
- **Contact the Société as soon as possible to file a claim for compensation:**
  - **by calling 1 888 810-2525 or**
  - **through a nurse who will open a compensation file for you during your stay in a hospital offering this service;**
- **Notify your insurer of any property damage caused.**

The Société will provide the forms and explanatory documentation needed to file a claim for compensation. The *Claim for Compensation* is also available in SAAQ service centres.

The Société provides help free of charge to assist in preparing a claim. A Société representative could go to an accident victim's home to help complete the form and submit the documents.

If information relating to a compensation claim is gathered in a hospital by a nurse, he or she will transmit the information to the Société electronically.

If a driver is involved in a collision with an inanimate object, an animal weighing over 25 kg or an unoccupied vehicle, and the owner of the damaged property or his/her representative is not at the scene of the accident or nearby, the driver must contact the nearest police station immediately to report the accident and give the above information.

Failure to comply is punishable by a fine.

AT THE SCENE OF AN ACCIDENT

The first motorist to arrive at the scene of an accident must:

- park his/her vehicle on the shoulder, some thirty metres away;
- warn other road users of the accident by turning on the emergency or hazard lights. Flares can be very useful for this;
- ask people to take up positions at a reasonable distance from the site of the collision, in the best location to warn traffic in all directions;

- turn off the ignition of the cars involved in the accident and see that no one smokes because of the danger of fire or explosion;
- look to see if anyone has been injured and administer first aid if capable. Otherwise, handling the injured must be avoided;
- report the accident by telephone to the nearest police station, specifying to the best of one's ability the location of the accident, and the number of injured victims and damaged vehicles.

Never move an injured person unless there is imminent danger of fire or collision with another vehicle.

FIRST AID

A prudent driver should always have a first-aid kit in the vehicle and follow these instructions:

- **Injuries:** while awaiting the arrival of ambulance attendants or a physician, stop the flow of blood through pressure applied with a pad, a thumb or a hand, if qualified to do so. Cover the injury with a clean dressing and a sturdy bandage. If necessary, apply a tourniquet.
- **Burns:** use a clean dressing to protect the burned area from exposure to the air and cover with a bandage. Never break blisters or remove a victim's clothing.
- **Other precautions:** keep the victim warm and comfortable under a blanket. Do not give anything to eat or drink to an accident victim who is unconscious or could be bleeding internaly. Otherwise, wet the person's lips and give sweet warm tea or coffee, a little at a time.

Chapter 6

OFFENCES AND FINES

*T*he Québec statute governing traffic matters is called the Highway Safety Code. Drivers should know that payment of a fine is equivalent to an admission of guilt; failure to pay can lead to prosecution before the courts.

In addition to fines for specific violations, demerit points may be entered on a driver's record.

The following table shows some Highway Safety Code offences and corresponding fines for passenger vehicle drivers.[4]

OFFENCES AND FINES

LICENCES TO DRIVE

OFFENCE	FINE
Failure to carry one's driver's licence, learner's licence, probationary licence or restricted licence	$30 to $60
Failure on the part of a licence holder to inform the Société within 30 days of a change of address	$60 to $100
Knowingly giving false or misleading information on a licence application	$300 to $600
Driving a vehicle on a public roadway without holding a licence of the corresponding class	$300 to $600

---

4 The main offences that concern heavy vehicle users are listed in *Obligations of Heavy Vehicle Users* available from the Société de l'assurance automobile du Québec.

Driving a vehicle despite a revoked or suspended licence, or suspension of the right to obtain a licence, for a reason other than demerit points or a driving-related criminal offence	$300 to $600
Driving or having custody of a vehicle after having consumed alcohol, if the person is under the age of 25 or if he/she has held for less than five years a learner's licence, probationary licence, licence for a moped or scooter (class 6D) or farm tractor (class 8)	$300 to $600
Allowing vehicle operation by someone who does not hold a licence of the corresponding class or who is under penalty for another *Criminal Code* offence	$300 to $600
Driving a vehicle despite a revoked or suspended licence, or suspension of the right to obtain a licence, due to an accumulation of demerit points	$600 to $2,000
Driving a vehicle despite a revoked or suspended licence, or suspension of the right to obtain a licence, due to a conviction for a driving-related criminal offence	$1,500 to $3,000

VEHICLE REGISTRATION

Failing to carry one's registration certificate, certificate of liability insurance or of financial responsibility, proof of the duration of a vehicle load or a copy of the lease contract	$60 to $100
Failure on the part of the registered owner to inform the Société within 30 days of a change of address	$60 to $100

Operating a motor vehicle fitted with a licence plate corresponding to another class of vehicle or one that was issued for another vehicle	$200 to $300
Installing an imitation licence plate or one that was issued for another vehicle	$200 to $300
Failure to return one's licence plate to the Société following registration suspension	$300 to $2,000
Fabrication of a false licence plate	$600 to $2,000

VEHICLES AND ACCESSORIES

Operating a motor vehicle that is not in good condition	$60 to $100
Operating a motor vehicle that is not equipped with two rearview mirrors	$100 to $200
Operating a motor vehicle or a combination of vehicles that is not equipped with at least one brake system in good working order	$100 to $200
Operating a motor vehicle on a public roadway that is equipped with substandard tires	$200 to $300
Operating a motor vehicle on which the brake system has been modified or altered to reduce its effectiveness	$200 to $300
Removing or altering a seat belt, or rendering it useless	$200 to $300
Deactivating an air bag	$300 to $600
Operating a motor vehicle equipped with a radar detector	$500 to $1,000

Modifying, defacing, rendering illegible, replacing or removing a vehicle's identification number without prior authorization from the Société — $600 to $2,000

TRAFFIC

Failure to use a turn-signal light to signal the intention to pass another vehicle	$30 to $60
Braking suddenly without reason	$30 to $60
Leaving a child under age 7 unsupervised in a motor vehicle	$60 to $100
Failure to use low beams within 150 metres of an oncoming vehicle, the vehicle ahead or on a sufficiently lighted road	$60 to $100
Driving a motor vehicle on a public roadway without wearing a properly fastened seat belt	$80 to $100
Driving a motor vehicle with a passenger under age 16 who is not secured by a seat belt or restraint device that meets standards	$80 to $100
Failure to yield the right of way to a pedestrian facing a green light or crossing on a white or flashing pedestrian signal	$100 to $200
Following another vehicle at an unsafe or unreasonably close distance	$100 to $200
Failure to obey traffic control devices on a public roadway	$100 to $200
Increasing one's speed when being passed or about to be passed	$200 to $300
Zigzagging to overtake vehicles	$200 to $300

Passing a bicycle in the same traffic lane without sufficient space to do so safely	$200 to $300
Passing on the right, except to overtake a vehicle making a left turn or a vehicle about to exit	$200 to $300
Crossing a solid line to overtake a vehicle	$200 to $300
Failure to stop more than five metres away from a school bus or minibus when its flashing lights are operating	$200 to $300
Failure to stop in either direction for a school bus or minibus when its flashing lights are operating	$200 to $300
Drinking alcohol in a motor vehicle: • driver • passenger	$300 to $600 $200 to $300
Operating a motor vehicle for a wager, stake or race with another vehicle, other than in a rally approved under the *Act respecting safety in sports*.	$300 to $600

SPEEDING

Unsafe speed or an act liable to endanger
life, property or public safety $300 to $600

Speeding offences:

Basic fine: $15

• Additional amount for each full 5 km/h
  exceeding the limit:

From 1 to 20 km/h: $10
From 21 to 30 km/h: $15
From 31 to 45 km/h: $20
From 46 to 60 km/h: $25
From 61 km/h or more: $30

OFFENCE	FINE
Example 1	
Speed limit: 50 km/h Recorded speed: 75 km/h Excess: 25 km/h **Fine:**	$15 + $75 = $90 (5 X $15)
Example 2	
Speed limit: 70km/h Recorded speed: 120 km/h Excess: 50 km/h **Fine:**	$15 + $250 = $265 (10 X $25)

MECHANICAL INSPECTION

Putting a vehicle in need of minor repairs back on the road after 48 hours without proving it meets *Highway Safety Code* standards	$100 to $200
Putting a vehicle in need of major repair back on the road without proving it meets *Highway Safety Code* standards	$300 to $600

MOTORCYCLES, MOPEDS AND SCOOTERS

Failure to remain seated while riding or to hold onto the handlebars at all times	$30 to $60
Failure to wear a helmet	$80 to $100
Failure to ride in staggered formation when travelling as a pair or group	$100 to $200
Riding between two lanes of vehicles moving in the same direction	$100 to $200

BICYCLES

Riding a bicycle without mandatory accessories, or without a white reflector at the front and a red tail-light at night	$15 to $30
Failure to ride astride a bicycle or not holding onto the handlebars	$15 to $30
Riding a bicycle between two lanes of vehicles moving in the same direction	$15 to $30
Carrying a passenger on a bicycle not equipped with a designed seat for that purpose	$15 to $30

Failure to ride single file when travelling as a pair or group	$15 to $30
Failure to travel on the far right-hand side of the roadway, with the flow of traffic	$15 to $30
Failure to obey traffic rules or traffic signs and signals	$15 to $30
Failure to ride on a cycle path or lane that is part of the roadway	$15 to $30
Modifying, defacing, making illegible, replacing or removing a bicycle's identification number without prior authorization from the Société	$30 to $60
Wearing headphones or earphones while cycling	$30 to $60
Holding onto a moving power-assisted bicycle or being pulled by one	$30 to $60
Riding a power-assisted bicycle on a public roadway when under age 18 without a licence authorizing the use of a moped or scooter or failing to respect the conditions and restrictions of this licence	$100 to $200
Failure to wear a helmet while riding a power-assisted bicycle on a public roadway	$100 to $200
Riding a power-assisted bicycle that fails to comply with the *Motor Vehicle Safety Act* and the *Highway Safety Code* on a public roadway	$100 to $200

FOOT SCOOTERS

Failure to equip a foot scooter with the necessary brake system	$15 to $30
Use of a foot scooter at night that is not equipped with the necessary reflectors or reflective material or failure to wear clothing or an accessory on which reflective material has been affixed	$25 to $50

PEDESTRIANS

Failure to obey traffic signs or signals	$15 to $30
Crossing a public roadway other than at nearby intersection or pedestrian crosswalk	$15 to $30

Printed in March 2007
by Imprimerie Offset Beauce Ltée
in Sainte-Marie (Québec)